W9-BXX-092

 Like Birds in Black and White

by Miriam Raz–Zunszajn

©2014

Translated by Rachel Sela

Like Birds
in Black and White

©2014
by Miriam Raz-Zunszajn
All Rights Reserved

Translated to English
from the original Hebrew (*K'Tziporim B'Shachor Lavan*)
by Rachel Sela

Published by:
MORESHET

The Mordechai Anielevich Memorial
Holocaust Study and Research Center

Givat Haviva
Doar Na Menashe 37850
ISRAEL
Tel: 972-4-6309257 • 972-4-6309204
www.moreshet.org

ISBN #: 978-1495492334

All rights reserved. The author retains all copyrights in any text, graphic images and photos in this book. No part of this publication may be reproduced or transmitted in any form or by any means, electronic or mechanical, including photocopying, recording, or any information storage and retrieval system, without permission in writing from the author.

This book is dedicated to my children– Osnat, Eldar, Shaul and their children. You are the light, the joy, and the reason for existence, and my source of strength. Your support and encouragement gave me the courage to reveal my memories to the masses.

Why my book is titled "Like Birds in Black and White"

Our home in Poland was located very close to the synagogue and Jews wrapped in black and white talitot (prayer shawl) and tefillin (phylacteries) would always pass by our house on their way to prayer.

Then, much to my surprise, one of the Shabbaths at the beginning of May 1942, the Jews of the village gathered in front of our home, crying out to heart of the heavens, instead of going, as usual to synagogue. The large crowd begged the Creator of the Universe to help Father and the delegates of the community, who were about to desecrate the Sabbath on account of their fateful mission.

To me, these men looked like giant birds in black and white, that no God, even the most callous, would be unable to refuse their pleas for help. Still today, their cries echo in my ears at night, and there no one pays attention.

I am the sole survivor of all the Jews from Wereszczyn, who remembers their cries, and worries each year the Kaddish memorial prayer is said on their behalf, and hopes that the coming generations who read this book will continue to honor their memory. We are their Kaddish.

■ *Miriam Raz-Sonszajn Winograd*

Acknowledgements

This book would not have seen the light of day without the people who assisted me at each of the stages of its writing. Thank you to Osnat, my daughter, who devoted nights and days to helping me, correcting, editing and experienced the writing of this book with me– which moved us both and brought us much closer.

Thank you to the many friends that read the manuscript and encouraged me to publish it: To Zvika Dror, to Naomi Alex, to Tova Adiv, to Nechama and Mordechai Rosenzweig, to Talma and Dan Sharon, and to Dan Shavit, who read the book, was inspired, and completed the linguistic editing.

Thank you to Amira Hanani and Mario Rappaport, the people of "Moreshet", whom without whose help, it would have been difficult to publish this manuscript.

Thanks to Shimon Cohen, my friend, who assisted me in solving every issue connected to the computer, which – from time to time – left me with no hope for salvation. And to Mordechai Hareven, a faithful over the course of many months.

Special thanks to Shaul Kenaz who took on the graphic layout of this book upon himself, and did the job with all his heart.

Table of Contents

A House in the Village

Gathering Clouds

Friday, the first of September 1939. Ominous dark clouds cover the sky. Lightening, thunder and rain. The faces of my parents are an even deeper grey than the clouds. "War!" My parents say, and judging by their expression I understand that war is something very menacing, although I don't know exactly what it is. I'm already six years old and today was supposed to be my first day in school, but I'm not there. Evidently it's all because of this war that arouses both my curiosity and my fear. My parents are very troubled and are listening for the sound of cannons amidst the bursts of thunder. I'm very confused: I know what prayer to say when there is thunder from the sky, but what should I say against the thunder of cannons? What exactly are cannons? What can they do to us? Why do they worry my parents so much? Can cannons cause fires like thunder and lightening do in a storm? Mama and Papa are occupied with their problems and I feel I shouldn't bother them with my questions and my fears. My little brothers don't really understand what's happening. They go on playing their usual games and I envy them. Cuddling up in Grandma's apron doesn't provide the comfort that it usually does. Due to worries about the war even the preparation for

Shabbat are being made offhandedly. Instead of the festive atmosphere that usually accompanies the welcoming of the Shabbat Queen in our house, today there is an atmosphere of tension, of sadness, anxiety and uncertainty. Polish marching songs are being played on the radio, songs of pride in our heroic soldiers who are fighting the Germans. I actually like the songs and I learn them quickly because I hear them many times during the day. Mama is very afraid that Papa will be taken to fight in the war even though he isn't really fit for combat. Mama's worries intensify my own fear of the war.

In the evening the Shabbat table is covered with a festive white tablecloth as it usually is, the *Chalah* (the Shabbat bread) has its own special covering, the silver candlesticks glitter as always, but the lighting of the candles is completely different. Grandma and Mama bless the candles, but the prayer is accompanied by bitter weeping and goes on and on for a long time. I'm deeply affected by Mama's and Grandma's weeping and I join them with loud sobs that were stored up inside me for hours. Mama and Grandma plead with He who dwells in the Heavens to keep us from harm and to keep Papa from having to serve in the army and fight in the war.

At the end of the meal we don't sing songs as we are accustomed to and I am very disappointed. The adults are withdrawn within themselves and the Shabbat atmosphere seems to be overshadowed by the heavy clouds. To me, the singing is always the best part of the Shabbat evening meal, both because I am an active participant and because I love hearing the whole family sing around the festive table. When I look at my family as they sing the Shabbat songs they seem to me to be surrounded by a special glow from another world, as though they are being uplifted on the wings of the Divine Spirit. But tonight the Divine Spirit isn't present. I ask myself– Where did it disappear to? What happened to it? Did the war hurt it in some way?

On this Shabbat day we remain hidden at home and don't take our usual walk. We detach ourselves from the outside world, but the outside world doesn't detach itself from us. The thunder of the cannons becomes louder and closer and no one knows what to expect once they reach us. Events follow one another so quickly that the world around me is like a whirlpool. Day and night, people carrying their belongings, pass our village on their way east. German airplanes flying low in the sky pass over our village with a deafening roar. Mother hides us under the beds. There are rumors that the planes shoot at everyone they see and in particular at the lines of refugees on the roads. Everything happens so quickly that the Germans conquer Poland even before Papa's conscription date. I am absolutely certain that this is God's answer to Mama's endless prayers.

Meanwhile, the world around us is changing. When the war broke out the Polish farmers were supplied with weapons, I don't know from where. They served in local militias protecting the interests of the Polish regime. The first act of these militias was to requisition a large portion of Jewish property for the sake of the war effort. They entered our homes and took anything they liked. In a short time the Polish militia disappeared and another militia took its place. This time the Ukrainian farmers were armed by an unknown source.

They wear red bands on their sleeves and become representatives of the Russian army, which, in the meantime, had invaded Poland. They too requisition as much Jewish property as they please for the sake of the Red Army's war effort. I am completely confused; I don't understand this war at all. Does the fact there is a war mean that various invaders will appear in the village one after the other? A number of Russian soldiers have come to the village and they're actually very friendly to the Jews. The soldiers are trying to convince Jews, my parents included, to flee to Russia. They claim that the Germans will be arriving in our area soon and when they do, they'll make life miserable for the Jews. Mama is trying to persuade Papa and Grandma to leave Poland while it's still possible and to migrate to Russia freely, but both of them are vehemently opposed to the idea. Papa isn't willing to give up the assets that they both worked so hard to amass over the course of so many years. Grandma, Papa's Mother, doesn't want to go to Russia because her memories about Russia are not good. During the First World War, the Germans didn't harass the Jews, and they even defended them from the plundering Russians. Papa and Grandma are not willing to leave Wereszczyn and move to a strange place and begin everything all over again. The reign of the Ukrainian Militia, under the patronage of the Russian army, was replaced by the new rulers who appeared in the village – the German army. According to the Molotov–Ribbentrop Pact, the Russians would retreat eastward as far as the Bug River, and we, living in the area to the west of the Bug would be left under German rule.

The column after column of refugees that moved east at the outbreak of the war are now flowing back westward to Poland under German occupation. I don't know why they're coming back, or if they are really the same people, but they look terrible. Their appearance is repulsive. They are filthy and they emit a bad odor. Their clothes are ragged. Their eyes are blank and expressionless, as though they've lost all vitality. There are some among them who are so thin, that it's frightening to look at them. Some of them are carrying their belongings in enormous sacks tied to their backs and others are harnessed to a small wagon holding their property. They're all stooped over and I don't know if it's because of the weight they're carrying or because of the despair they feel. They look as though they're starving. Mother offers them a large pot of tea and biscuits she baked to have in the event that we, too, would join the processions. She offers food to everyone passing by and who is willing to accept it. Mother feels that helping others is the most important of the commandments and she never misses an opportunity to carry it out. When I see all those miserable, homeless people trailing through our village, I think that Papa and Grandma were right when they refused to leave home and go to Russia with the Russian soldiers. We might now have been homeless and miserable looking, like these people passing through our village, and that would be terrible.

A short while after the German invasion, a new order is established in the village. Horrifying posters denouncing the Jews appear on the village walls. The Jews are described as filthy monsters who spread contagious diseases. I remember one poster in particular, on which there was a picture of a very ugly Jew whose long beard was crawling with gigantic lice. A large caption was printed above the picture, saying, *"Jews are lice, Jews are Typhus".* My father also has a beard. Though I've never seen lice crawling in it, nor have I ever seen anything resembling that poster among his Hasidic friends. I ask my parents what that poster means. They explain to me that it deliberately slanders the Jews in order to make the Polish people hate them. The Poles in our area don't particularly like the Jews as it is, and the German propaganda intensifies and legitimizes their hate. Many of them are prepared to cooperate with the Germans despite the fact that the Germans are their enemy and the conquerors of their land. I'm only a six-year old girl, but I understand that we are presented as something bad, as inferior people, outcasts and different from other human beings. I look for the human difference in me, in my parents, in our Jewish neighbors, but I don't succeed in finding it. I examine my reflection in the mirror and try to see in what way I'm different from the Polish girls, from the girls that were my friends until recently. I don't find a thing; my hair is as light-colored as it was, my eyes are still blue, my face is like the faces of many Polish children. I ask my Mother what's wrong with me and with the other Jews in the village, and she has no answer for me.

Every day a new poster appears on the walls of the houses forbidding the non-Jews in the village to have any contact with us. The Polish villagers are forbidden to buy anything from Jews or to befriend them in any way because they spread disease, they swindle and they exploit. Each day there are new decrees obligating the Jews to pay fines, to do forced labor, and to relinquish their property. From the time the Germans entered our village the Jews have had to ransom their very lives almost daily. In order to differentiate between Jews and non-Jews, the Jews are made to wear white bands on their sleeves with the word *"Jude"* inscribed in the center of a blue Star of David. The white band actually appeals to me and I envy the adults because only they have to wear them and children like me don't have to. Mama is very pleased by this. She says I look like a Gentile, and without the band the Germans won't discern that I'm Jewish.

Savta Luba **Zunszajn** with brother Nathan in her arms. To the right, brother Yosef, age 7. Behind her stands Miriam, age 9. Father is in the doorway of the house.

With the arrival of the Germans our lives change entirely. My father is consigned to forced labor together with other Jewish men from the village. This is the first time in my life that I see my father, an honored Yeshiva (Talmudic Academy) student, holding a shovel and being pushed roughly by the German soldiers. What happened to the respect everyone had for him up to now?

Miriam, age 2 (left) | Miriam, age 4, and brother Yosef (right)

Brother Nathan in the bedroom

Has the accepted order of things suddenly been changed? Will there be only chaos from now on? I don't understand these changes and I have no one to ask about it. Mama and Grandma are so immersed in their prayers for Papa's safe return that I'm afraid to disturb them, because if something does happen to him, God forbid, it will be my fault. I feel that the questions about respect and honor that are occupying me aren't important right now. The basic values I was taught to respect have been utterly abandoned since the Germans came to our village.

Face to Face with a German

One winter evening in 1940 we hear loud knocking on our door. It doesn't sound at all friendly and Mother looks through the slit in the door to see who it is. Before she realizes what is happening, the door is forced open and a good-looking young man wearing a green uniform and shiny boots, his hat brandishing the insignia of a skull, bursts into the house. He demands to see Papa. I don't know why, but the adults believe that the Germans won't harm women and children, and therefore Mama is always the one to conduct negotiations with them, in order to protect Papa. The young German shouts at her: he wants Papa and not her. When Papa approaches him, he demands of Papa two kilograms of tea and one of black pepper immediately. These two articles are absolutely impossible to obtain in our village. When Papa tries to explain this to him, the German's handsome face takes on a very cruel expression. He grabs Papa by the collar and thrusts him to the floor. Gentle Papa, the Talmud student, who never raises his voice to anyone, who is always genial to others, is now lying battered and humiliated on the floor of our home and says nothing. I burst into tears, stamp my feet and scream. I become hysterical with fear. My entire body begins to tremble as though I am in the throes of some madness. Grandma is holding my two little brothers close to her and trying to keep them from seeing the drama unfolding in our house. Mama, as usual, takes charge and decides on a plan of action. I don't know where she finds the daring and the strength. She approaches the German and tells him that he won't find what he is looking for in our house even if he beats us all. Humiliating Papa won't enable him to grow leaves of tea or grains of black pepper. Better to send Papa to the houses in the village to try to find tea and pepper there than to beat him.

Mama is a beautiful, soft-spoken, logical woman. When she speaks to him the German's face softens a little. I don't know whether her character or her beauty influenced him more. He takes her advice and commands that Papa go into the village to find the tea and the pepper. Mama wanted to protect Papa by prompting a way for him to leave the house, and she succeeded. She knew that he had no chance of finding what the German requested anywhere in the village, but she preferred to deal with the problem herself on the assumption that the German would probably not hurt a woman. I continue to scream. I have no control over my fear. My screams annoy the German and he commands Mama to shut me up. He doesn't understand why I'm quivering so much and screaming and crying and asks Mama what happened to me and if I'm insane. I don't know how Mama dared, but her answer came as a surprise to the German. "Try to imagine", she says to him, "that you are in my daughter's position and someone does to your father what you did to hers. Wouldn't you react the same way?" The German looked somewhat confused and surprised by Mama's answer. He says nothing and sits down to wait for Papa. I get diarrhea and ask Mama to hurry and bring my potty because I can't control it. We have no bathroom in the house, only in the yard, and children aren't taken out to the outhouse on cold winter nights. Mama sits me down on the potty next to her, which is quite close to where the German is sitting. I don't know whether she did that deliberately or not. Perhaps she hoped it would make him leave. The situation was ridiculous. The German is sitting opposite a little girl on a potty and is waiting for tea and pepper that her father is supposed to bring him. The odor from my potty spreads all over the house and all the windows are closed because of the bitter cold outside. A member of the super race is sitting within the foul smell that is being dispensed by a Jew.

Approximately an hour after Papa had left the house; Mama approaches the German and offers him a proposition: "Since it will take my husband a long time to attain the tea and pepper that you requested, because he has to go from house to house, I suggest you return to wherever you come from, leave us your address, and tomorrow you will have what you asked for or a sum of money equal to the price of those commodities." I don't know what convinced the German to accept Mama's offer, perhaps the promised money or perhaps the stench that permeated the entire house. He wrote the document that Mama requested and left our house. Mama waited a long time after the German left before going out into the village to look for Papa. She wanted to be certain that the German wouldn't change his mind and return to us. Papa and Mama returned home close to midnight. I waited for them anxiously, cuddled up to the warm oven. I didn't agree that Grandma put me to bed before my parents returned. I don't know how Mama and Papa solved the problem, whether they actually found tea and pepper, or paid ransom money. I was left with a strange souvenir of my first face-to-face meeting with a German. Every time I saw Germans entering the village, I would develop diarrhea.

My Mother Wrapped in Fabrics

The textile shop, the source of our income has been closed, by command of the Germans, ever since they entered our village. Most of the merchandise had been stolen from our store even before the German invasion. They simply completed the robbery. We have no other source of income and the money we had saved for a rainy day is gradually dwindling away. Hunger is beginning to irritate us. My father is the head of the community, and is not free to worry about the economic problems of our single family. He is totally occupied with issues of the whole community, and therefore the burden of supporting the family falls on my mother's shoulders. My parents succeeded in moving some of the merchandise from our store to a secret basement in our house. This enables us to obtain food in the meantime. Mother wraps her slender body in fabrics and wanders through the neighboring villages to trade the fabrics for food. This is forbidden and illegal and Mama is risking her life each day. In order not to be caught she leaves the house after sundown and takes indirect side roads to the villages. This is very frightening for me. I worry most when she has to go through the Christian graveyard of the village. I've been afraid of the graveyard for as long as I can remember. I imagine skeletons rising from their graves, pitchforks in their bony hands, and attacking Mama, stabbing her in every part of her body. The skeletons frighten me even more than the Germans. Every time she sets out on one of these trips my anxiety returns. She usually returns after midnight and I lie awake waiting for her while the rest of the family sleeps. My anxiety for Mother is extreme and no one is able to help me overcome it, not even Grandma, Papa's Mother who lives with us and has been taking care of me ever since I was born. I am the firstborn in our family and my love for my Mother is boundless. Although I have two younger brothers whom Mother loves very much, I always feel that her feelings for me are special and she loves me more than all the rest.

Mother was orphaned at birth since my grandmother died in childbirth. Mother had a difficult childhood with her step-Mother who didn't pay any attention to her, and with a foster family that was impoverished due to the mother's illness, and wasn't able to provide for her properly. When she finally succeeded in raising a family of her own, nothing was more precious to her than that family which she takes great pride in and is very devoted to. Mama tries to give us everything that was lacking in her childhood. She and I share a kind of special world of our own, perhaps because I am a girl. I am pampered and enveloped in love. I don't know why, but in her prayers Mama always asks of He who dwells in the Heavens, that if anything happens to our family, at least Masha, her beloved daughter – meaning me, will survive. She showers me with attention, dresses me in the nicest clothes, braids my hair with loving care, bedecks me with ornaments and puts salt in my shoes to guard me against the evil eye. She teaches me many different prayers, and on the Shabbat she reads me stories from a huge book called *Tzena U'rena* ("Come Out and See"), written especially for women. She teaches me blessings to assuage my fears, and I even know a blessing to protect me from the huge dogs belonging to the Poles, that sometimes pounce upon children. Mother also teaches me many feminine skills. I enjoy learning them and am very proud that at the age of six I already know how to knit and embroider. Mother likes to sing and she sings beautifully. When she sings I always get the feeling that she has sprouted wings and is floating in the sky like a bird. I feel that she wants me to join her in the sky and therefore teaches me countless songs in Yiddish and Polish; current songs, sad songs, songs from her orphaned childhood. Her voice entrances me. The songs she sings to me are quickly imprinted in my mind and deep into my heart and I remember them to this very day.

The dire conditions we are living in demand increased effort and thought in order to feed the family. Many products, which we had used daily before the war, have disappeared completely. One has to invent suitable, edible substitutes for them. Grandma and Mother's creative instincts have been working overtime and they've been concocting many such substitutes. For example coffee – a product that cannot be found in the market for any amount of money – is now made from roasted acorns. After the acorns are roasted they are ground in a coffee grinder and the result is a brown powder, which greatly resembles genuine coffee. I'm not familiar with the taste of the coffee because children don't drink coffee, but the grown-ups say that the taste is bearable.

Sugar, which has become a rare commodity in our parts, is made in our kitchen from turnips, and it's much tastier than saccharine which is generally used as a substitute for sugar.

Extracting sugar from turnips necessitates cooking them for a long time, using large amounts of fuel, which is also becoming quite rare, but how can you raise children without sugar? Salt, an absolute necessity, is unavailable, and has no substitute such as saccharine. I don't know where Mother learned how, but she succeeds in producing salt. She brings home a green, repulsive and spongy mixture, which she cooks for hours, until it becomes white and tastes very salty. Grandma and Mother also change the ingredients of bread in order to increase the quantity. They add mashed potatoes to the dough, because flour is rationed out to each family in very small insufficient quantities, while potatoes are still available. I love to participate in all the activities in the kitchen. I learn all sorts of culinary tricks from Mother and Grandmother. I am fascinated by everything they do. Bread mixed with potatoes is delicious when it's fresh. A day or two after it's been baked it becomes as hard as a stone and you can break your teeth eating it. In order to keep the bread edible, they bake small amounts more frequently. I get permission to bake a small loaf of bread for myself and eat it when it's still warm. As far as I'm concerned the taste is divine.

As the days pass and the war continues our hunger increases and it's more difficult to cope with. The lack of commodities that we were accustomed to before the war, but were considered luxuries, isn't such a hardship. However, hunger for basic food, like bread and other such staples, is hard to bear. When you're hungry you can't think of anything but food. Even I, who knows how to sail off on the wings of my imagination to numerous places and events in order to forget the growling of my stomach, don't always succeed in overcoming my terrible hunger pangs. My brother Yosef is swelling, he's grown a big pouch. They say it's from malnutrition. I don't want to develop a huge stomach like my brothers. I'm now willing to eat all sorts of strange things that I previously wouldn't touch for all the money in the world. When I recall that Mama used to pay me money to eat nourishing foods, I feel very ashamed. Today I'm even willing to eat grass when my hunger drives me mad. Only those who have experienced hunger are capable of understanding the meaning of the word 'starvation' and all the things people are capable of doing for one small slice of bread. I've already begun to understand from experience that war is a terrible thing, especially for the Jews.

I can't even dream of going to school, for which I was so eager. There is no school in the village that accepts Jewish children, not the Polish schools and not the Ukrainian schools where Mama tried to register me. I am even prepared to go to *Cheder*, the Jewish religious school– but that's only for boys. Having no other choice, my parents look for some other solution so that I will get an education. Several families in our situation, that is with children of school age, got together and hired a private teacher named Fela. Fela was a well-educated woman, one of the refugees from the beginning of the war. She remains in our village with her little son and will now be our teacher. She has nowhere to return because her house was destroyed by the German air raids, and also she has no other way of making a living. The possibility of earning a living by teaching saves her and her son from starvation, and saves us from boredom and idleness. Four hours every day our house becomes a school for the Jewish children my age. We are taught to read and write in Yiddish and in Polish, and we also learn arithmetic. Our teacher says that after one year of our lessons we will be on the same level as children who completed four years of regular school. I don't know if that was really so, but I read and write Polish and Yiddish without making any mistakes, to this day.

The Meatballs that were *"Treifed"*

One winter day in 1942 my mother somehow obtains a small amount of kosher meat. This was during a period when we were truly starving. Bread and meat were even extremely rare commodities in our household. Mother asks Grandma to prepare a large quantity of meatballs from the small amount of meat that she has obtained, so that each of us can get a taste of the delicacy. We children are excited about the activity in the kitchen, which reminds us of better times. Mother, who as usual, is occupied with searching for the bare necessities of life, is not at home, and Grandma, queen of our kitchen, is totally in-charge. A wonderful fragrance spreads through the house, and we become increasingly curious. It's a long time since we've smelled anything like this. Grandma expands the mixture in every way possible, she adds a lot of bread, onions, parsley, garlic – and the mixture expands and expands. Our eyes are glued to Grandma's hands and when she begins to roll the meatballs, I ask her to let me join her. Grandma doesn't consent. She doesn't want to take the risk of spoiling even one meatball. She fries pan after pan of fragrant meatballs and then pours them into a ceramic cauldron made just for that purpose. Our mouths are watering and we are now all in a festive mood. We are waiting impatiently for our parents to return home so that we can sit down at the table. Our patience lapses and Grandma barely succeeds in keeping us from snatching the ready meatballs. She doesn't give in to us this time. She insists that the whole family eat together. When Mama and Papa finally come home. We all sit down to eat. Mama's face suddenly grows pale. I have never seen her so angry with Grandma. She asks her furiously, "In which frying pan did you fry the meatballs?" Grandma doesn't understand why Mother is asking her such a strange question. She has no doubt that she fried the meatballs in the proper frying pan, and answers that of course she fried them in the frying pan for meat. Sadly, Mother shows her that the meat frying pan is still hanging on its hook. Grandma grabs her head with both hands. It is impossible. She couldn't have made a mistake. She's certain that she used the proper frying pan. Mother carefully examines all the frying pans and then declares unequivocally that the one Grandma used for the meat patties is actually for milk products. The meat patties are therefore not kosher and forbidden to eat. Grandmother looks at us full of mercy. Her attempts to convince Mama that since the milk frying pan hadn't been used for half a year it's permissible to use it to prepare meat are in vain. She pleads with Mother to allow the children at least to eat the meatballs so as not to disappoint us. Her request doesn't move Mother from her determined stand. She forbids us to eat the un-kosher meatballs. Our disappointment knew no bounds; we had so eagerly looked forward to that meal. The house is still full of a delicious smell, but we have to be satisfied with the potatoes and the scent of the meatballs, which were delivered to our Gentile neighbors. In times of shortages one does not throw such a treasure into the garbage can. Over fifty years have passed since then, but I'm not capable of forgetting the story of the meatballs and the disappointment in not being allowed to eat them when we were so hungry. My beloved Mother, who was willing to selflessly sacrifice herself for us, left us hungry because of her deep religious beliefs.

Work Permits

Despite the hunger, the monetary fines impoverishing us all, the various edicts that are renewed almost daily, the adults– and among them my parents– claim that life is somehow bearable. I definitely agree with them. Even in these circumstances brought upon us by the turmoil of war, I find many joyous moments. I try to hide my little joys from the adults, because I'm afraid they'll be angry with me if they discover that I'm floating along in imaginary and enchanted worlds in these difficult times. Even in wartime birds continue to sing as they always have, and I sing to myself along with them. Flowers continue to bloom in the spring exactly as they did before the war, and I have had a special affinity for flowers ever since I became aware of their existence. I almost burst with joy whenever I see a flower. Everything around us is full of color and intoxicating scents, the world is so beautiful that even though my stomach is growling with hunger, I don't succeed in shutting off my feeling of excitement. I take part, with all my heart, in the joys and the beauty the spring brings with it.

I'm very attentive to what is happening around me and try to find something positive in every possible thing. I think that in spite of the upheaval the war has caused, life is still beautiful.

I'm still living in our house with my beloved family, no one has been driven out of the village, no one has been murdered, and I thank God for that in my own way, in prayers that I, myself, compose. There is a common Yiddish saying: "We will outlive the Germans", and I hope that's the way it will be.

From the beginning of the year 1942 relentless rumors have reached us; rumors about Jews driven out of their homes and concentrated in closed off districts, called ghettos, within the cities. There are also rumors about mass murders, including women and children, but no on one is prepared to believe them. It is simply unthinkable that innocent people would be randomly murdered in cold blood, including women and children. A terrible fear has begun to take root in my heart, but I keep it to myself. I try to quell my fears with all sorts of imaginary heroic stories, and I also convince myself that if the adults aren't taking any precautionary measures, the situation probably isn't so terrible. At the moment everything is quiet at home. Although Papa, as head of the community, is inundated with demands from the Germans, in particular the necessity to present precise lists of the entire Jewish population in the village. Everyone attributes that obligation to the German penchant for strict order. They don't see it as a warning of danger or as a cause for fear. The number of taxes the Jews of our village are required to pay increases every week. These taxes are called "contributions", and despite the fact that the Jews are already impoverished, they succeed in scraping some more from the bottom of the barrel in order to save their lives. The Germans are evidently aware of that quality of the Jews and exploit it unrelentingly. Since our village is located in a very remote area, the Jewish inhabitants try to convince themselves that such a God forsaken place will be passed over by the Germans. Many think that it's not worth the effort for the Germans to deal with such a small group of Jews. No one even imagines that there is meticulously planned, systematic plan for murder taking place. Most of us try to believe that nothing will probably happen to us.

In spite of the relative optimism, our parents prepare us for the possibility of escaping into the forest, in the event that the Germans decide to drive us out of the village and move us to the ghetto. They dress us in several layers of clothes and don't allow us to undress at night. When going to bed we only take off our shoes and lie down fully clothed. There is always one adult who stays awake. We, the children, find this over-dressing very funny. I, who am very slender and agile, am suddenly fat and clumsy. It's difficult for me to run about and play wearing so many clothes.

Sleeping with our clothes on is a shocking experience for us, in particular because it used to be unthinkable for us to do: Who would have dreamed that it's possible to get into a clean white bed wearing the clothes we played in all day? Suddenly all sorts of things that were once absolutely forbidden are now permissible. With all the pleasure there is in this and the feeling of adventure, I'm keenly aware of my parents' anxiety. I've been infected by that anxiety in its full intensity.

In the beginning of May 1942, a rumor was spread by the Germans that every Jew of working age must carry a work permit with him *(Arbeitausweis)* proving that he is employed in useful work. The German regime will not tolerate parasites under its rule. A Jew caught without such a permit will be subject to exile, or worse – to execution. The Jews of the village are overcome by anxiety. The door of our house is never closed, everyone comes to ask Papa's advice and ask him to act quickly. Real or fictitious places of work for the entire adult Jewish population must be created urgently. In the event of a German inspection there must be an up-to-date list of the Jews working. Since their very lives may be at risk, the required permits must be attained with utmost speed. The Community Council meets very frequently at our house, but no one suspects the Germans of setting a clever trap for the Jews of the village. Everyone is certain that if they obtain the required permits, their lives will be saved.

On Friday Papa receives an official message informing him that he is responsible for arranging work for all the Jews in his jurisdiction, and for providing proof of these jobs with work permits. There will soon be a surprise German inspection and all the parasites eating at the expense of others, (meaning those without work permits), will be severely punished. A tremendous burden has been placed on Papa's shoulders; the lives of the entire community are in his hands. The German announcement is made at the end of the week, and the inspection may take place as soon as Monday, not leaving any time to arrange the permits. The government offices are closed on Sunday. They're open on Saturdays; but on *that* day the Jews would be desecrating the Shabbat, which is only permissible in a matter of life or death. What can be done? All the Jews are afraid that if they don't apply for the work permits during the Shabbat, there will be a catastrophe. Papa calls an emergency meeting of the Community Committee for consultation and invites several Jews who are well versed in Jewish Law. They decide to approach the rabbi of the community to determine if applying for the permits can be considered a matter of life or death. I don't remember how long and in what manner the discussion of the wise men took place, I just remember that I curled up in my parents' bed and prayed endlessly to He who dwells in Heaven to help us. That Shabbat eve was a sleepless one, and the following Shabbat was so horrific that I shall never forget it. It's been engraved deeply in my heart for the rest of my life.

Like Birds in Black and White

Shabbat morning. My parents rise at dawn after lying awake all night. Papa doesn't wear his special festive coat as he has worn on every previous Shabbat. Instead, he wears a suit and a tie, like secular men. He also doesn't prepare his prayer shawl and phylacteries as he always does. He prepares for a trip. I don't understand what's happening. I had never before seen my parents desecrate the Shabbat. It is all beyond my comprehension.

An enchanting spring day; the smell of flowers, birds chirping, warm pastoral serenity. It's always pleasant to get up on the Shabbat morning and go to pray or just take a walk outside. But this time, contrary to every other Shabbat, Jews are not going to the synagogue. They are gathering outside our house, cloaked in their payer shawls. My father, the rabbi and two community representatives get into a wagon harnessed to two horses, say good-bye to all the people gathered there and start out on their way. All the rest of the Jews begin a quiet prayer, which gets louder from time to time, and becomes a heart-breaking cry. The women and children burst into tears. Everyone is imploring He who dwells in Heaven, to guide the delegation of Shabbat desecraters to success in their mission of saving the lives of everyone in the community. The situation makes me shudder. I'm absolutely certain that even if God lives far from here, He must hear the prayers of the men and the voices of the women and children begging Him for salvation. All my life I have heard that God is merciful and compassionate. How then, can I imagine that He won't help us after hearing prayers of great devotion, coming from the depths of our hearts?

The wagon moves in the direction of the city Wlodawa and the group of men wrapped in their *taleisim* (prayer shawls), resembling a flock of giant white birds with black stripes, turns in the direction of the synagogue to continue their prayers. The women and the children remain standing as though rooted to the ground, looking toward the heavens and continuing their endless silent prayers. In the depths of my heart I wait for some sign from the heavens answering our prayers, but no such sign is forthcoming.

The delegation, headed by my father, worked hard all through the Shabbat. Its people ran from one German clerk to another, who exploited the naïve belief of the Jews that their lives depended on the work permits. Their work is hard and exhausting. They beg, coax and bribe. At the end of the day they succeed in returning

These documents, issued by the German authorities, verifies that the holders – Miriam's father (top) and Miriam's mother (bottom) are engaged in work that is essential and they must not be harmed. Miriam found these in a pile of work permits lying next to the mass grave.

Wereszczyn, certifying that all those obliged to work are actually employed in useful work. After acquiring the work permits, a feeling of serenity descends upon the community. Everyone believes that he is now safe from being exiled to forced labor, or from an even worse fate. They each have documents certifying they are employed in work essential to the German government, and that this assures them they will be allowed to live.

Miriam's Mother,
Henia **Zunszajn** Winograd

Miriam's Father,
Alter **Zunszajn** (Photo from 1942)

The Vow of a Nine-Year Old

On Wednesday, the 14th of May 1942, about two weeks after the acquisition of the prized permits, we wake up early in the morning to the terrible sound of tank motors. We don't know what it means. Since the phenomenon is unusual and arouses our suspicions, we all immediately rise, dress quickly and anxiously await what is to come. Mama serves us the little food found in the house. Suddenly the door is forced open. Germans and Ukrainians serving in the German army order the adults to gather near the village church, where everyone's work permit will be checked. No one suspects that there is anything threatening about this examination of the permits. Everyone has a permit and there is no reason to worry. Mama quickly prepares the food for lunch in pots and places them on the stove ready to be cooked when she returns. Papa, who is head of the community, leaves the house immediately, without waiting for Grandma or Mama, because it is his duty to be the first one there. Grandma doesn't have the patience to wait for Mama and she follows Papa to be near her beloved and only son. Her heart foresees disaster. The children aren't obliged to go, we aren't the age to work, we don't have permits and thus we are allowed to remain at home. The fact that the children are allowed to stay at home reassures the adults that nothing bad is about to happen.

I am terrified. I have the feeling that something horrible is going to happen and I ask my Mother not to leave me alone with my two small brothers. I don't want her to go to the Germans, I'm afraid of them. I suggest to her that the four of us hide in our secret basement, where the precious belongings of the family are hidden, and come out only when the Germans finish their inspection and leave the village. Mama, of course, doesn't agree that Papa be there without her, only with Grandma, and she explains to me that the wife of the head of the community can't absent herself from the inspection. I hold on to her with all my strength, my fingernails are imbedded in her flesh, I cling to her and when she tries to free herself from my grip, her arms are scratched. I refuse to leave her. Mama presses me to her breast, soothes me with a big hug and a kiss and leaves the house. It never occurred to me that that hug and that kiss would be the last I ever received from my mother.

Time drags on; I don't understand why Mama doesn't return. She knows how afraid I am. I was also made responsible for my two little brothers and it's hard for me to keep them occupied for such a long time. They lose patience and begin to go wild. I can't continue to sit in the house. In spite of my great fear, I decide to go outside with them. Maybe I'll find someone who can explain to me what's happening to our parents and why they aren't returning home. Outside there is a frightening silence. The Gentile villagers have disappeared entirely, as though the earth had swallowed them up. I see another group of frightened Jewish children, who don't know what to do with themselves. They also don't know anything about their parents and are very worried about them. In our childish logic, in our intuition, which is apparently sharper than that of the adults, we sense that danger is lying in wait for us and decide that it pays to hide until our parents return. We all sneak into the hayloft of one of the farmers and bury ourselves in the hay. Anxious and frightened we sit quietly in the hay. No one dares to speak or cry, paralyzed with fear, waiting for what's to come.

I don't know how long we were hiding when suddenly the door of the hayloft is opened and a Jewish woman, mother of 4-year old twins who are hiding with us, comes in. Her sudden appearance creates a commotion and fear. What she tells us is terrible. It might be that some of the children would have been saved if she hadn't come. She looks as though she's lost her mind. Her hair is unkempt, her face and arms have signs of fresh bruises, her eyes bulge with an insane glimmer, as though they are about to burst out of their sockets. Her appearance is so strange and frightening that it's difficult to recognize her. She shrieks with heart-rending cries when she finds her children among us, "They're going to kill us all; I don't want to leave you as orphans, come to die with me and Papa". She takes their hands and begins to stride with them in the direction of the assembly of all the Jews in the village. She doesn't pay any attention to the other children in the hayloft who now don't know what to do, or to the horror that her words arouse, completely deaf to the weeping and shrieking, in a daze she, seeing nothing she leads her children to their death. In spite of the horror her words arouse in us, all of us leave the hayloft and follow her. If one mother claims that we should die with our parents and even succeeds in coming to get them, all the mothers must feel that way, but didn't succeed in coming to get their children. We all understand that we must join our families so as not to be orphaned, and we all advance toward the place where the Jews are gathered in order to die with our parents.

I'm the eldest in our family and already nine years old, my brother Yosef is seven and my little brother, Nathan, is only four. The responsibility for their welfare is mine and I give one hand to each of them, exactly as the mother of the twins did and walk with them towards where our parents are. As the older sister I feel that I must bring them there come what may, and I hold on to them with all my might.

I don't completely understand the meaning of death, According to the reactions of the adults when someone dies, I understand that it is something frightening and sad, but I have never had any personal experience with death and have never seen a dead person.

Suddenly, little Nathan revolts and begins to shout and to cry that he doesn't want to die, he doesn't agree to go with us. We stop and I don't know what to do. Perhaps he's right, but I didn't have Mama's permission to leave him alone, he is, after all, just a little boy, only four years old! I hold him tight and cry with him. Seven-year-old Yosef urges me to hurry; he doesn't want to wait any longer. When he sees that I'm not managing with the little one, he takes on the demeanor of an adult and says to me, "I'm not staying with you, I'm going to Mama and Papa to die with them". He frees his hand from mine, looks at me with his big, sad eyes as though he knows in his heart that we will never see each other again, and he leaves. I'm incapable of coping with both of them and I have no choice but to let Yosef go. Now there is only Nathan and I, and from a feeling of responsibility towards my little brother I try with all my might to make him come to die with our parents, just as Yosef did, but he refuses to go. I struggle with him as long as I can, but he eventually succeeds in freeing himself. I'm left alone. I cry and feel acutely guilty that I wasn't able to hold on to my little brother and bring him to our parents. How will I explain his absence to my mother?! Alone and frightened I continue to walk in the direction of my family and all the other Jews of Wereszczyn. There are German and Ukrainian soldiers, armed with bayoneted rifles, standing all along and on both sides of the main and only road of the village. As I walk along, I beg the soldiers to kill me. I'm afraid, I can't go on, and I don't want to see my parents killed before my eyes. I want to die here and now in the middle of the road. None of soldiers pay any attention to me. My pleas fall on deaf ears. I don't understand why they don't shoot me. I loudly declare that I am a Jewess and if their intention is to kill Jews, so why don't they kill me? Maybe they don't believe me because of my Arian appearance, or perhaps they're so evil that they want me to see my parents' death? I continue to walk and the closer I come to the place, the more frightened I become. I'm very close. I can already see the cross on the spire of the church, and now I see the church with the crosses in the cemetery. I know that the Jews and my family are gathered behind that cemetery.

Soon I will be with them. Suddenly I sense that I hear my mother saying, "My beloved daughter, don't come any closer, because here only death awaits you. Run away and hide. You must save yourself. Someone from our family must survive as a reminder that we existed. A scion (descendant) of the Zunszajn family must remain alive! The word *"scion"* becomes engraved in my very being. I hear it continually in Yiddish and in Polish. It's like a hammer endlessly pounding in my head. It becomes a mantra of my mother's unequivocal demand. The magic word, *"scion"* instills in me strength that I never knew I had and enables me to do things I never imagined I could do. I feel that I must obey my mother's command. I must survive, come what may!

Instead of continuing in the direction of my parents who are several meters away, I turn around and run to the nearest house. I plead with the Poles living there, to hide me quickly. I tell them that I must stay alive as my mother commanded. They look at me as though I were mad. They see in me only trouble for them. Despite the fact that they know what is happening outside, they are frightened by my invasion into their house and want to get rid of me as quickly as possible. I don't understand what they find so frightening about me. I am the same girl I was yesterday. Just a few days ago I played 'hopscotch' and 'catch me' with their daughter. Now they seem not to know me at all. They have no room in their hearts for a little Jewish girl who just wants to live. They drive me away and mockingly tell me that Jews live in the house across the road. An eighty-year old, sickly Jew lives there. The Germans let him be because it would be a shame to waste a bullet on him. "You can go to him. He will surely greet you with open arms".

I'm afraid to leave their house, as the street is full of Germans. I return and beg the Polish family to let me stay with them until the evening, just until it gets dark. My repeated request arouses their anger and they drive me out with blows. Having no choice, I run as fast as I can to the Jew's house. There I find an old man named Shmariah who has often been a guest in our house at festive holiday meals. I sit down beside his bed. He really is happy to see me and welcomes me warmly. Shivering with fear I ask him what's going to happen, what are they going to do to my parents, are they going to simply kill them like the Polish woman said? But he has no answer.

Time creeps on, there is a paralyzing silence everywhere, and every sound is alarming. How lucky that I have an adult next to me, even if he is ill and helpless. I'm able to find some consolation in that, despite the fearful situation. Suddenly shooting is heard nearby. I understand that these are the shots that are murdering the Jews of Wereszczyn, among them, those who are more precious to me than anything, the members of my family. All the waves of fear I have experienced until now are nothing in comparison to the fear that overtakes me now. I want to disappear, to die together with them, and I also want to live, to hide, but I don't know where. The old man understands what is happening. He also fears for his life, but he can barely move, and just continues to lie in bed. I run about the house frantically looking for a hiding place. I discover a cover in the floor of the kitchen resembling the door to the secret basement in our house. I know that the basement cover is very heavy, but I must open it no matter what. Finding strength I have never known before, I lift the basement cover, go down the ladder underneath and close myself in. The basement is dark, moist and frighteningly unfamiliar. I feel lost there. But the fear of death overcomes all my other fears. I'm alone. There is no one to tell me what to do. My familiar world has disappeared all at once. What now? Who do I turn to? What's going to happen? How do I live from now on, without a family, without a home, without everything that made up my world just a few hours ago? How do I live without the guidance of adults? How do I live without a mother and a father?!

I don't know how long I've been in the basement; everything is confused in my mind and an endless number of questions rattle in my brain. Suddenly I hear the old man shouting upstairs, "Fire! Fire! The house is on fire! Little girl, hurry and get out of the basement before you are burned alive". I don't understand what is happening: just a short while ago I found shelter in this basement and I thought I had a good hiding place for a while, and I already have to leave?! I'm afraid to leave and afraid to stay. I must decide quickly what to do. Remaining in the basement means being burned alive, going outside means getting a bullet in my head. What is better for me, please Mama, send me some hint, send me a message telling me what to do and how to behave.

My indecision ends quickly. Smoke from the fire begins to penetrate into the basement. I must get out of here before I suffocate. With the little strength left in me I push the heavy basement cover with my head and escape. The flames are already licking the walls of the house and the smoke is too thick to bear. With difficulty I find the door and choking from the smoke, I burst outside, cross the street and run madly into the fields. I want to get away from this dangerous area as quickly as possible; I don't want to get caught. Running, I come to a swampy area, fall and get up, fall again and get up again. I run on and on and on with whatever strength I have left. My entire being is intent on running in order to get as far as possible from the place threatening my existence.

I have uncles living in the neighboring village. I run in the direction of that village to find shelter with them. A Polish farmer, driving his wagon, who sees me running in panic through the fields, calls to me. I approach him, frightened, perhaps he, too, is a bad person. He asks me where I'm heading and why I am alone without an adult. I tell him that the Germans killed my parents and I want to get to my uncles in the next village. He looks at me compassionately and suggests that I return to Wereszczyn with him, because the Jews in the neighboring village were killed the day before and no one is alive there. I'm in shock. How does he know that they were killed yesterday while we heard nothing about it? Did our Polish neighbors know about the massacre and hide it from us? Had we been told Jews in our area had been killed yesterday, we would have fled to the forest at night and my parents wouldn't have attended the murderous inspection which led to their deaths. I'm undecided and helpless: the outcome of returning to Wereszczyn may be death, there is no place left to go and there is no adult to tell me what to do with myself. All the decisions are now on the shoulders of a nine-year old. What should I do? I'm afraid to remain here in the field alone at night. I therefore decide to go cautiously back to Wereszczyn. Despite the friendly impression the farmer makes, I don't accept his help. My instinct tells me that I shouldn't trust the Polish people. It's clear to me that danger lies in wait for me in Wereszczyn, but I feel I must go back there. I want to see what is left of my family. Perhaps some of them escaped just as I did. Perhaps I'll find my little brother who slipped away from me.

Slowly and cautiously I approach the village through the fields. It is now twilight. The intoxicating fragrance of spring blossoms is in the air. There is a pastoral serenity all around, as though nothing had happened today, as though the slaughterers hadn't slaughtered. The tanks with the murderers had already left the village. They accomplished their mission and everything supposedly had returned to the way it was beforehand. Instead of first going to my house, I go straight to the pit of death, to look for signs of life. I get close to the back of the church and the Christian cemetery, to the place where the Jews had gathered just that morning. Instead of living people I see a new huge hill. It had previously been the ruins of a well and now it became a gigantic mass grave. Piles of clothing are spread around the grave. The victims were stripped of their clothes before being murdered. They were tortured and humiliated. There was also a big pile of documents, the work permits that were supposed to insure the lives of the Jews. The permits stated in black and white that the holder mustn't be harmed because he is essential to the German government. It was clear that the writing was worthless. The permits are stamped with the symbol of the Third Reich and signed by the German officials of the Labor Office in Helm and in Wlodawa, but it is all a deliberate deception. Their clever fraud worked on the naïve Jews exactly as the Germans predicted. There was no opposition and no attempts to escape.

I don't know why, but the first thing I do there is to look through the pile of permits. I'm looking for the permits of my family and I find those of Mama and Papa. I don't succeed in finding Grandma's permit. I pull out my parents' permits, which carry both their photographs and press them to my heart. It's ironic that the only thing left me from my family are the very same work permits that are strewn around the place where they were murdered. The permits accompany me through all the years of my wanderings during the war and after it. They are a testimony to the terrible German fraud, and they are all that is left of my family, of my home, and of the life I previously had.

Now I go on to the pile of clothes to look for the clothes of my family. I don't find a single article of my family's clothing even after a tiresome search, except for my brother Yosef's hat. A great hope awakens in my heart: if their clothes are not among the pile of the dead, that's a sign that they are still alive and are perhaps waiting for me at home. Before leaving the place, with the document pressed to my breast and my brother's hat in my hand, I vow beside the huge grave, that if I, the only surviving scion of my family, will succeed in remaining alive until the end of this terrible war. I will do everything in my power to immortalize the memory of my family and of the Jews of Wereszczyn. I will not allow this pit to remain secret and unknown. In her message my mother demanded of me to survive in order to keep the family's memory alive and I intend to fulfill that demand, come what may.

I run to our house as fast as I can, without imagining that the reason I didn't find any of their clothes was that the clothes of quality had already been stolen by the villagers before I arrived. The path home passes the burnt-down homes of Ukrainians living in the village. They had cooperated with the Russian army in 1939 when they invaded us. I don't even notice that a large part of the village of my birth has been burnt to the ground. I am only concerned with what is happening to me and what I will find at home. It was later made known to me that the Germans had exact information on the activities of every individual in

Wereszczyn, despite its being a remote village. All the Ukrainian men who were believed to be Communists were murdered along with the Jews of Wereszczyn. They were accused of cooperating with the Red Army, and the Germans knew which of them had been in the militia and had worn a red band at the time of the Russian invasion. The Germans did not exterminate the wives, children and animals of the Ukrainians. Today there is no trace of any Ukrainian community in Wereszczyn. Their memory, just as that of the Jews, has been completely erased.

The Looting

I arrive at our house and hear voices from inside. My heart beats wildly. I'm certain these are the voices of my family. But it is an illusion. The house is full of people, but not my family. They're Polish villagers. Everything is upside down; I can barely recognize my own home. The cupboards have been emptied, the clothes have disappeared, the bedding and the dishes are gone, and even the cooking pots with the food that Mama had prepared have been taken. There is no semblance of the tidy house I left just a few hours ago. Our neighbors, our Polish friends, are looting everything they can lay their hands on. They examine every crevice, every crack and search for treasures that the *"Zydym"* hid away. They're not embarrassed when they see me, and they don't stop the plundering. My fate and that of my family don't interest them. They're behaving coarsely, as though everything that belonged to us is theirs to choose. When they notice that I'm wearing several layers of clothing, they take off as much as they can. I am left with just one thin dress. My entire world collapses. Who can I believe in? Are all people bad, and not just the Germans? If Papa's friends are looting our house and me, then they are also a source of danger for me, and I must beware of them too. To whom can I turn now? Until now I was used to being guided by Papa and Mama or by other adults. Now there is no living being in the world to guide me, and I am only a nine-year- old girl!

Suddenly the Postmaster of the village appears in the doorway. I don't know how and why he came here. I have never seen him visit our house before. He calls me aside and suggests that I hide somewhere, because the Poles are liable to report me to the Germans to get the payment being offered for reporting Jews. He tells me that the house is going to become the post-office of the village, because the previous post-office located in the Ukrainian section of Wereszczyn was burnt down together with all the Ukrainian houses. I understand that this man has my interests at heart and that I should take his advice and hide, but I don't know where. I don't want to be caught or reported to the Germans after I succeeded in escaping from them. I find it difficult to understand the world I live in: the house I grew up in, the place where I always felt most secure has suddenly become dangerous for me and I mustn't remain there if I want to stay alive. The village where my grandmother was born, where my father grew up and where I was born, is now a dangerous place for me to be in, and the people who just yesterday were considered friends are now enemies.

It's already very dark outside. I, who was afraid of the dark even when I had a mother and a father, am doubly afraid now. Though the dark also has the advantage of making it easier to hide, that fact doesn't in any way relieve the terror I feel being alone in it. I would like to disappear somehow– to see, but not be seen– like in the fairy tales. Sadly, fairy tales don't belong in this new world. I must be practical and find a hiding place quickly if I want to survive.

The "friends of our family" are so preoccupied with looting our house that they forget I exist. I succeed in getting out of the house with relative ease. I'm already outside, but what am I to do now? Where can I hide? The instinct to survive guides me to the only refuge I know that is near home. We have a hayloft in our yard with a great deal of hay and straw. I sneak inside the loft, climb up on a pile of straw and dig in, hoping that I won't be found here. When night comes and all is quiet outside, I suddenly hear a noise in the piles of straw not far from me, and my blood runs cold. The thought that comes to me is that after looting all our possessions the villagers will come now to annihilate me. Evidently they did follow me after all, and now they will catch me. But I am overwhelmingly surprised when I discover that two Jewish neighbors, with their children, who are my age, are hiding in the straw as I am.

In the midst of the horror, sorrow and confusion of my situation, this comes as a tiny ray of consolation. At home I learned that Jews are our brothers in every way and that they help one another in troubled times. In my childish innocence, I believe that these two Jewesses will agree to take me into their care, if I just ask them to. I approach them and ask them to take me with them wherever they go, and I promise to be a good girl, to behave nicely, and to do anything they demand of me. They are both very tense and frightened, and they promise me to do anything I ask, if I will just be quiet now, since every sound is liable to reveal their hiding place. I stop speaking and curl up in my corner in the straw, crying softly for my terrible loss. I am crying for my family, my home, my freedom, for my entire world that was so suddenly and cruelly taken from me. The tears keep coming and there are so many unanswered questions that give me no peace. Do people feel anything after death? And if they do, what do they feel? What is my family feeling right now? Are their souls here with me? Do they see my great distress? Maybe it would be better for me to die now so that I could be with them? And if I survive now, will I really meet them when the dead are resurrected? Grandma used to tell me that when the Messiah comes all the dead will be resurrected and it will be possible to meet all one's loved ones who had passed away. I think about my friends, girls my age who died. Will I also meet them when the dead are resurrected? Will they still be little girls as they were when they died? I see them now as little angels with wings, fluttering in the sky. I envy them. They have no sorrows and fears as I do now.

Mother left me her will and I'm committed to it, but life is now an almost impossible mission for me. Suddenly a thought comes into my mind, that if I survive and want to tell about the Jews of Wereszczyn, I don't even know how many Jews there were in the village. I try counting them by passing mentally from house to house and noting how many people lived in each house, and

I check it again a number of times in order to be sure I'm not making a mistake. In the end I arrive at the number 320. So many people buried in one grave. I'm horrified by the thought that they are pressing on and squashing each other. I fervently pray to God in the hope that my family is lying at the top of the pile, I don't want their bodies to be squashed, I don't want masses of dead bodies to be pressing down on them because maybe even after death it hurts.

I'm not capable of imagining that suddenly Mama, Papa, Grandma and my brothers turned into something that can't think or feel, like objects or stones. But I'm not certain whether a stone has feelings or not. Every additional thought about the dead members of my family and everything connected with their death intensifies my sobbing. I can barely succeed in keeping quiet. I want to scream a terrible scream that will reach the Heavens, a shriek that will reach God. Where is He? Why is He silent? Why doesn't He come to His senses and stop all this evil being inflicted on the Jews, His chosen people, His children that He created in His image? Due to all the thoughts running through my mind and to all my crying, I forget to say the prayer, *Shema Yisrael* ("Hear O Israel") which up to now I always said with Grandma before going to bed. In the end I simply fall asleep.

The two women who were near me in the hay, evidently waited for the moment that sleep would overcome me. Then they secretly left, taking their sons with them, without my being at all aware of it. Looking back on it today I understand that they didn't want to burden themselves with an additional child who wasn't even related to them. Even without me, their chances of survival in that hostile environment were minimal. At the time, I, of course was unable to understand their behavior. The frustration and helplessness that overcame me – when I awoke and discovered I had been deserted – were abysmal. Jewish women, our good neighbors, broke their promise to me. What happened to the Jewish brotherhood I had such faith in? I couldn't forgive them for disappointing me. I felt betrayed and deceived. I then concluded that all people are bad and are not to be trusted, not even Jews.

What Price for the Head of a Jew?

I've been lying awake in the hayloft for a long time. I'm again utterly alone. The Jewish women and their sons are gone. Darkness and despair surround me and I have no idea what this new morning will bring. I await it with dread. Dawn is slowly penetrating the darkness; rays of light are filtering through the cracks in the wall. But I'm surrounded by endless hay and loneliness. The lighter the hayloft becomes, the greater the darkness within me. Frightened, filthy and very hungry, after a full day in which no food came to my lips, I again wonder what to do in this impossible situation. How long can I endure without someone's help?

It's early in the morning. I can tell by the light penetrating through the cracks in the wall. I can hear agitated voices outside the hayloft, people are running about and their shouts are growing louder. It quickly becomes clear to me that everyone who saw me at my house yesterday and paid no attention to me is now looking for me. I have no doubt that they will soon find me and I must find some way of escape. My situation seems hopeless and I decide to turn to the only person who might help me, judging by my experience with him yesterday – the Post Master. But how am I to reach him? Where will I find him now without being detected? I cautiously start walking in the direction of my house, which is close to the hayloft and is now serving as the village post office, but the villagers waylay me. Within seconds, I am surrounded by people who were considered "friends of the family" only yesterday. They are now determined to hand me over to the Germans. They chase me with pitchforks and heavy sticks, as they would chase a dangerous wild animal, and I fail to understand why they're doing this to me. How can a little nine-year old girl, who was born in their midst, do them any harm? What is clear to me, however, is that if they do catch me they will lead me to my death. I try in every possible way to escape them, but there are so many of them and they're stronger than I am. They capture me like wicked witches are captured in fairy tales.

The Germans pay one hundred zloty and ten kilograms of sugar for a Jewish head. Evidently, that is a sufficient price for the Polish villagers to make the effort to capture and deliver me to the Germans. I will never forget and never forgive the people who rushed around on that cruel hunt, along with the horror of the pitchforks pressed against my body. I had the feeling that all the hatred of Jews that had been imprinted in the Polish people for generations was now concentrated in this heartless hunt for a nine-year-old girl who did them no harm– whose only crime was being Jewish. Apparently they feel that any means are justified in attaining the aim of cleansing the village of its Jews. To justify their behavior they call me names, beat me, and rain curses on my head, and on my family, and on my whole accursed people. I'm a dirty Jew, a disgusting and useless creature, who has the audacity to try to resist them. They capture me along with two young Jewish men. This is a real treasure for them: thirty kilograms of sugar and three hundred zloty for the three of us.

There is no German or Polish police station in Wereszczyn. In order to receive the prize for capturing us, they have to bring us to Urszulin, a village six kilometers from Wereszczyn. Our captors leave us in the care of the three strongest men in the village, who, with the aid of gigantic clubs, are supposed to bring us to the Germans, to our deaths. From the experience of my short life, I already know what I can expect from the Germans and I try to escape along the way. All the schemes my childish mind devises in order to get out of the grip of my captors are in vain. They don't even allow me to move my bowels in private. My every attempt to escape is accompanied by curses, insults and blows from a club. The three young men who are from my village are guarding us so carefully that we have no possibility of escaping them. The distance to Urszulin seems to me to be endless, although it's only six kilometers. I ask myself if this is the last time I'll ever walk along this road. The landscape around me is so familiar, so beautiful now. It is really enchanting. Everything is green. The fields are already speckled with spring flowers. The buzzing of insects sucking the nectar of the flowers sounds like string instruments playing softly in the serenity of the countryside. The trees, which were bare all winter, are already budding and their shade of green is so fresh, so soothing.

We arrive at Urszulin and my heart pounds so forcefully that I fear it will explode. I've been here many times with my father, and never before was it in any way frightening to me. On the contrary, I have pleasant memories of the place. We would visit my uncle who had a dairy and was an expert on "yellow" cheeses. We would eat and drink high quality dairy products and bring a stockpile home. I used to like inserting my finger into a hole of the yellow cheese and eat around the holes.

Now this place fills me with fear. I'm sure that the angel of death is waiting for me here. When we arrive at the police station, the young men, who brought us here, come to a halt. Here they lose their status of authority, and look small and submissive standing beside the ruling Germans. With us they had the upper hand and treated us cruelly. Here they stand aside quietly, and wait for one of the Germans to notice them and award them their prize for the three Jews they brought.

The sun has already moved a long way and it is now late in the morning. The Germans are outside doing gymnastic exercises with bare chests. They are smiling, and look relaxed and very healthy. On the surface they are ordinary people. I ask myself whether they have human hearts like all human beings, or are they "angels of death" dressed like humans? Are they going to suddenly stop their pleasurable activity and come to murder three children in cold blood, only because they were born Jewish? These thoughts are rushing through my mind. I must do something to save myself, I must survive, go on living, and I think quickly about how. I raise my eyes and look around me, like a trapped animal trying to escape from the trap. At the other end of the building, I notice the chief officer of the Polish Police, an old acquaintance of my father's. In a flash, my instinct to live, or perhaps my mother's soul, tells me I must approach him. I have nothing to lose now. With lightening speed I detach myself from the group, run to the Chief of the Polish Police and beg him to do something to prevent them from murdering me. I also tell him that I'm the only one left alive in my family, and about my about my mother's message telling me that I must survive in order to keep their memory alive. The Chief of Police looks at me with eyes full of compassion and promises to try to save me. He approaches the Head of the German Police, exchanges a few jokes with him, and then points to the three little Yids, meaning us, and suggests letting us go. He tells the German officer that it would be a waste to besmirch themselves now in the murder of only three, when the plan is, according to his knowledge, to exterminate all the Jews of the area by September, and then in any case we would be exterminated as well. The Germans consult with one another for a short time and decide to accept the suggestion. They clearly don't feel like interrupting their enjoyable gymnastics in order to deal with us. They tell the Polish Chief of Police to let us go. During this entire episode, which seems like an eternity, I am gripped by overwhelming fear. I'm trembling so uncontrollably, that I feel as though my body is being torn apart. I keep repeating, *"Shema Yisrael"* over and over again. My parents told me that Jews say that prayer before death, and I feel that my life is about to end.

In the very instant the two boys hear that the Germans are releasing us, they disappear from view. I am left alone with the Germans and don't know what to do with myself. All the resourcefulness that had helped me survive up to now suddenly leaves me. My life was just given to me as a temporary gift, but now I don't know what to do with it. Where shall I go and who can I turn to? Who will be willing to take care of me? I know that if I keep standing here near the Germans, they're liable to change their minds and kill me, but I have nowhere to go from here. I begin to cry from somewhere deep inside me. I want my mother! I want her to tell me what to do now, where to go and who to turn to. I feel lost and alone in the world; I have no more strength to fight for my life. I want someone to help me, to give me some advice.

Suddenly, as though sent by my mother, a Jewish woman from Urszulin appears. She was known in the entire area for her dire poverty and the great number of children she had. She takes my hand and says: "Don't cry, it's alright. If we can find food to feed nine mouths, we'll find a piece of bread for a tenth as well. Come home with me. You can live with us." This woman, named Esther, was my Savior. It was as though she had been sent by a guardian angel watching over me, not just this once, but also later on.

At this time, the Jews of Urszulin are still living in their own houses. They have not yet been subjected to any harsh edicts, and the atmosphere in the village was relatively peaceful. I don't know if they were aware of what was happening to other Jews in the area. Rumors came to Urszulin about the atrocities carried out against the Jews of Poland, but it's convenient to ignore them. They understand that they're living on borrowed time, but for the moment the situation is normal. In any event, they can't do very much to prevent what may happen to them. Escape is just about impossible in such hostile surroundings. The Poles cooperate with the Germans and report every Jew caught trying to find a safe haven. For families with little children it's tenfold more difficult. They have almost no chance of escaping. Since most of the families in Urszulin have young children, they are all sitting in their closed up homes, awaiting what is to come. I sit in Esther's house, curled up in one of its corners and crying my eyes out. I miss my family more and more every day. I feel that I can't bear the pain of my loss. The adults are understanding, and forgiving. They say that I need time to adjust to my new situation. The children are less tolerant. They don't understand why I don't want to play with them, why I keep to myself, and cry all the time. Is it beneath me to associate with them? They think I'm a snob and an incorrigible cry-baby, and they snub me.

Esther and the Policeman

Several weeks have passed since I arrived in Urszulin and started living with Esther's family. Those weeks have passed routinely with no extraordinary occurrences. In Urszulin as a whole, life has been routine and uneventful. I pray in my heart that this is the way it will continue to be. I want to sit quietly in my corner and cry without being disturbed. I don't want to be touched.

Esther, who took me into her home, is gentle and understanding, something I am very grateful for.

Suddenly, early one morning, we hear the rumble of tanks surrounding the village. The sounds are exactly like those we heard in Wereszczyn before the roundup of the Jews– and in accordance with my story about the massacre in Wereszczyn, it was clear to everyone that our turn had come. We get dressed in tense silence, but we don't flee, because there is nowhere to go. Trembling with fear, we all wait for our fate to be decreed. Will there be a massacre as there was in Wereszczyn? We are not allowed much time to speculate. We hardly manage to get dressed when the Germans and the Ukrainians in German uniforms break into the house and begin to push us outside with their bayoneted rifles. I refuse to leave. I tell the Ukrainian who is trying to push me out that I know what awaits me outside and I refuse to move from the house. My words arouse his fury; he aims the barrel of his rifle at me and begins to shout that he will kill me inside the house if that's what I want. Before he can press on the trigger I bolt outside in alarm. There's bedlam outside. People are crying, screaming, running back and forth, chased by the Germans and their partners, the Ukrainians, who push them with their bayonets. I run about within the confusion, not knowing where to run.

Suddenly I notice Esther. She is standing exactly opposite the entrance to the Polish Police Station. She is holding her baby in one arm and holds the hand of her limping son with the other hand. The little boy is my age. The Commander of Police, who rescued me just a few weeks ago, is standing in the entrance and watching what is happening outside. I don't know what Esther was thinking at that moment, but when she saw me, without a moment's hesitation, she put the baby down on the ground, released her crippled son's hand, grabbed me with both her hands and threw me over the fence into the courtyard of the Polish Police Station, shouting to me, "You are destined to live".

I don't understand what happened, it all happened so quickly. Within a fraction of a second I found myself in a completely different world. I'm outside the turmoil of death. Although only a fence separates me from that world, I feel relatively secure here, and I also sense a shred of hope. I don't understand why Esther didn't try to save one of her children by putting them over the fence. Why did she just try to save my life? But this isn't the time for questions of that sort– and there is also no one to ask.

The Police Commander doesn't reject me or chase me away. Instead he offers me his hand and asks me to stand quietly next to him. Both of us are standing near the entrance to the police station and watching what is happening on the other side of the fence. Fortunately for me, no one pays any attention to me. The pursuit of the Urszulin Jews and the turmoil it causes are over in a very short time. Suddenly everything is quiet, and then the shots annihilating the Jews are heard. Everything is being conducted exactly as it was in Wereszczyn. Evidently the Germans have a fixed, well-staged system, which they employ in all small villages. The massacre seems to be over, because in a short time we hear the tanks leaving, then, a troubling silence in the village. Perhaps the term 'the silence of death' would be more fitting. The people who gave me a home when my family was killed are no longer among the living. My new world was destroyed before I had the chance to become accustomed to it. What will happen to me now? What will the man who is now holding my hand and who has already saved my life once, do with me?

The Police Commander notices the distress I'm in and tries to reassure me. He promises me that he will try to arrange a place where I can stay now, for the time being, and that he will *not, under any circumstances,* deliver me to the Germans. Holding my hand tightly like a rescuing anchor, he brings me to a Polish house very close to the police station, to a lady called Kozlowska. She is a farmer's widow and has only one son at home, who is seventeen years old. An additional girl at home could be very useful to her and help with all kinds of tasks. The Police Commander leaves me in her hands, asking her in a mixed tone of request and command, "If anything happens to this little girl that I'm putting in your care, both you and I will die. Teach her our prayers, give her the name and identity of your family, and God will help you". He releases my hand and leaves without a word to me, not even good-bye. I don't understand exactly what is going to happen with me now, and he is already gone. I never again saw that noble man. I don't know his name or his history. Although after the war I heard the Germans had executed him, because of his Communist past. His actions taught me that not all the Poles are bad. There are good people amongst them. Even if they are few in number, they do honor to their country and allow me to continue believing in the good in people. He saved my life twice and was a great ray of light for me in the evil reality of the time. Apparently the story of the 36 righteous people in the world isn't a fairy-tale, but is rooted in real life. It's true that people encounter them, from time to time, in the hardest hours of their lives, as happened to me, and I am certain that the Polish Police Commander was one of them.

An Instant Christian

Mrs. Kozlowska treats me exactly as the Police Commander instructed. She changes my Jewish name from home – Masza – to the Polish name Marisia, and even gives me a new family name, her own family name. From that day on I am Marisia Kozlowska, the daughter of an aunt from a neighboring village, who was sent to help with the plentiful farmstead tasks. Mrs. Kozlowska explains my presence to her neighbors by telling them that her only son isn't capable of doing all the work on the farm and the household, especially ever since German soldiers came to live in her house.

Kozlowska has her son teach me how to make the sign of the cross, and to say the Christian prayers that are said after getting up in the morning and before going to bed at night. Within a very short time, less than an hour, I must change my identity, my religion, where I come from, and my name. I must say the Christian prayers on my knees, something that was absolutely forbidden in my religious home. The most important prayer I have to learn is "Our Father in Heaven" –"*Ojcze nasz*" and that "Father" is also a new God for me. I repeated that prayer so many

times that it has been engraved in my mind forever. Although
so much time has gone by since then, I still remember it word
for word and am able to recite it in my sleep. One room in the
Kozlowska home is rented to members of the German Police
Force and they move about the house as though it belongs to
them. I must constantly play my role of being a Christian, lest my
Jewish identity be revealed to the Germans living in the house.
My fair hair and blue eyes, symbols of the Aryan Race, are of
course very helpful. My appearance is that of a Gentile, but in my
heart I am a devout Jewess, tied to her heritage with all her soul.

The irony of fate is that I – the daughter of Alter Zunszajn, the
wise disciple of the Rabbi from Lubartow, and the daughter of
the pious Henja Zunszajn who fasted every other day to atone
for her sins, has to pray to the Christian God to watch over me. In
our home it was forbidden to mention the name of Jesus, because
it was considered a terrible sin, and now I must vocally request
His help from the moment I open my eyes in the morning. I'm
terribly afraid. I expect something awful to happen to me because
of my sinful behavior towards the Jewish God, and I'm certain
that He will teach me a lesson. All through my childhood I was
taught that we are punished the moment we turn to the God of
the Gentiles. It's an act of heresy according to the education I
received at home, and I know that heresy like mine is punished
by some terrible death, being burnt in Hell by boiling tar, and
that's what I expect to happen to me now. I am also afraid that
the souls of my mother and father, who probably see my sinful
deeds from up above, are deeply grieved. But in spite of my fear
of my Jewish God, I know that the only way for me to survive is

to become a perfect Christian, as I am being taught to be in the home of Mrs. Kozlowska. I must forget the Jewish girl I was up to now. I must forget my name, Masza Zunszajn; forget my home, my family, my mother tongue, and my heritage. I must erase my past immediately. Now, there is only Marisia Kozlowska.

The evening of the same day that the massacre took place in Urszulin, when our German tenants return from their work, I am introduced to them by Mrs. Kozlowska as the daughter from a poor house, who will remain with her for some time to help with the household tasks and with breeding the geese. Due to my Aryan appearance, I don't arouse their suspicion. They actually take a liking to me and with time, when they're in a good mood they play with me. Within days I become a perfect Christian, who even plays with the German soldiers, the murderers of her People, and perhaps of her own family. After every prayer I devoutly recite while facing the Cross so that the German tenants will hear me and be impressed by my devotion, I fearfully wait for my punishment by the Jewish God.

The nights are even more difficult for me than the days. I don't sleep at all...I'm afraid to fall asleep out of fear that in my sleep I will shout something in my native tongue – Yiddish, which the Germans understand well because of its similarity to German. I'm always tired and dizzy. The only place I allow myself to nap a little is in the meadow when I take the geese to pasture. That little nap in the fields keeps me from collapsing. According to what I learned at home, eating pork is a terrible sin, and I want desperately to avoid committing that sin, in order to atone for all my other sins. Therefore, whenever the farmer's wife serves me pork, I make all kinds of excuses not to eat it: my stomach hurts when I eat meat, it makes me nauseous; I'm not hungry now, etc. The farmer's wife doesn't care if I don't eat meat – it even saves her money. Most of the time, I eat bread, vegetables, potatoes and milk products. In this way I somewhat maintain my Jewish identity and I hope that I appease my parents and the Jewish God.

Most of my time is spent with the geese. I think a great deal about what I've been through and I also worry because I don't know what to do in order to assure my survival. It's clear to me that I won't be able to remain here much longer in the company of the German tenants without their discovering my true identity, but I have nowhere to go. When I feel very upset I decide to return to living among Jews, if there still are any in the near vicinity, without taking into account the danger in such a step. My most difficult moments are when the Germans touch me while we play together. Each and every one of them might have been the murderer of my family and that thought is unbearable. Under these circumstances I can't allow myself to falter and exhibit any hint of my true feelings towards them. It could cost me my life.

I ask Kozlowska to find out if there are any Jews remaining in the vicinity and explain that I miss being with Jews, and want to live among them in spite of the danger involved. I have no contact with the Polish Chief of Police. He's probably keeping his distance in order to be cautious. However, since I don't understand his distancing himself from me, I don't take him into my confidence concerning my plans. Actually it's convenient for me not to be attached to anyone. This way I have absolute freedom, within the limitations of my new life.

The Last Meeting

One day Kozlowska's son tells me he heard about a group of Jews living not far from Urszulin. That's wonderful news for me. The thought that I could again live among Jews, hear and speak my mother tongue – Yiddish – and that I might no longer be compelled to play the part of a devout Christian, makes me very happy. I don't ask myself if these Jews will be willing to accept me. I want to get away from here at any price and this seems to be my only chance. Altogether, everything connected to Jews seems so perfect to me now that I'm certain that they won't turn me away, that they will be happy to have me. I ask Kozlowska to send me to the place that her son discovered and ask if it's possible for him to accompany me there because I'm afraid to go alone. To this day I don't know if she was glad or sorry that I left. She said nothing. It is to her credit that she permitted her son to take me to my longed for Jews with the horse and wagon. The wagon trip put an end to the period of Marisia Kozlowska, the devout Christian girl. I don't remember how long that period was, but it was very difficult for me, and yet very meaningful.

I'm in the wagon, happy in the knowledge that I will soon meet with Jews, but I have no idea who they are. And once again I'm about to be surprised beyond belief. The boy stops at the edge of the forest, beside a Jewish wayside inn. I bid him good-bye, thanking him profusely, and he turns quickly to return to

Urszulin. It isn't desirable to be found in the neighborhood of Jews. He might even be suspected of helping them and that might cost him his life. I walk up the path leading to the inn and go inside.

To my great surprise I see Esther and her crippled son sitting beside the table. I don't believe my eyes. It takes me time to understand that I'm not imagining it or dreaming. It's real. I was certain that she was already among the dead of Urszulin, and here she is in the flesh, and even her son is alive. My happiness knows no bounds. We embrace, kiss, and cry in happiness and sorrow. Despite the fact that the acquaintance between us was short lived, I love this woman very much, and want very much to be near her. In the heat of my emotions I ask her to let me stay with her forever and be a substitute for my mother. I'm very much in need of this. In the course of our conversation I learn that the inn belongs to her mother and serves all those who come through the forest. Fortunately for Esther and her mother, the Germans haven't put their hands on the inn. Esther's mother has cancer and Esther helps her with all the housework and the work in the inn.

My request to remain under her protection is emphatically denied. She isn't willing under any circumstances to respond to my pleas. She claims I have no chance for survival if I remain with them more than one night. She says that despite the fact that she loves me very much and would happily adopt me as her daughter, especially now that all her daughters were killed, she won't do it for my own sake. My desperate attempts to convince her fall on deaf ears. She tells me emphatically that this is her final decision, and that I must stop working on her conscience because it's very difficult for her. I'm very disappointed, but understand that I must accept her decision. Esther asks me if I know of any Polish family that would agree to take me until the storm passes over, and if I do, she recommends that I go there for my own good no later than the next day. With tears in her eyes she tells me that I will be grateful to her for sending me away.

I feel that I must tell the story of how Esther remained alive after the massacre in Urszulin, so as to honor the memory of this wonderful woman. She told me the story that same evening. After the Germans drove the Jews from their homes, they crowded them into a large hayloft, ordered them to lie down in rows on the floor and shot them. In the turmoil of crowding into the hayloft, Esther managed to push her son into one of the piles of straw and she lay down with her baby as ordered. Volleys of machine gun bullets were fired at the Jews lying on the floor and after a while the place became quiet. The murderers had completed their mission. After affirming that everyone was dead, they left the building. Esther, covered with the blood of her baby was sure that she was dead, and so were the murderers. She felt what she imagined one feels after death. Her arms and legs could move, her heart was beating, but she didn't dare move because dead people don't move. When she finally did try to raise her head, she discovered that she was the only one alive. The blood of the baby in her arms had spattered over her and saved her. She realized that she had to get out of there before the farmers came to bury the dead as the Germans had ordered them to do. She pushed into the pile of straw where she had hidden her son and waited with him until nightfall, surrounded by the dead who included her husband and her seven children, who were later buried in a communal grave somewhere in Urszulin.

When night came she and her son fled from the hayloft to her mother's house, the inn, not far from Urszulin. I found them there several weeks later. I have no idea what happened to Esther after we parted. But her memory has been stored in my heart throughout my entire life. She was my lifesaver during very difficult times in my life. Despite her poverty, lack of education, and her simple life, she was noble in spirit and a good soul. She played a meaningful part in my survival.

After a night of frenzied dreams I open my eyes in the inn and see a small package lying beside me. It is only shortly after dawn, but Esther and her mother are already busy with all sorts of tasks. Esther asks me if I already know where and to whom I will go. I know about a possible place, but I don't tell her in order to stretch the time I'm with her just a little more. She makes me feel secure and loved and it's difficult for me to part from her. When she tells me I will have to leave her even if I don't have anywhere to go I understand that I have no choice and I don't have too much time to bask in the pleasure of her presence. I tell her that after searching and searching for an idea, I thought that the Bacher family who knew my family and live in Zalucze village might accept or find shelter for me somewhere.

The two women urge me to leave their house because there's no knowing what might happen in the very near future. The package they prepared for me contains a few slices of bread and it is wrapped in a cloth tied to a stick so that I can carry it on my shoulder. Esther instructs me how to conduct myself and how to get to Zalucze. She tells me read all the road signs and go in the direction they indicate. Wherever the arrow shows the direction to Zalucze, turn in that direction. She also tells me not to speak to anyone on the way, and if someone insists on knowing my name, or who I am, I continue to be Marisia Kozlowska, a Polish girl going to visit relatives. If I see some vehicle in the distance, or some other sign of Germans, I must hide in the fields. I should also beware of Poles because they are traitorous. I must try not to come in contact with anyone on my way to Zalucze. I'm afraid of going alone on unfamiliar roads. Esther's instructions also frighten me. What will happen if I lose my way or someone confronts me? Will I succeed in convincing them that I'm not Jewish? Will the people I chose to go to agree to accept me? I didn't ask them and what will I do if they refuse? But there is no other choice. If I want to remain alive, I must make the attempt. I set out on my way after a painful parting from Esther and her mother.

An Outsider

With the Bacher Family

Again I am alone on the country roads walking towards the unknown. What will happen to me now? Did I make the right choice? If the family in Zalucze isn't willing to accept me into their home, where else can I turn? I don't have any more acquaintances in this world, and I appeal again to my mother with a silent plea to ask for her help. I want her to influence the people I am going to now, not to reject me. I no longer have the strength to battle with my terrible fear and loneliness. The fragrance of the green fields and the pleasant summer sun somewhat relieve my tension. The world around me is so beautiful, that I'm not able to ignore it even in this difficult time. Here and there I steal a glance at the landscape around me, although I devote my attention mainly to the road before me. At this time of year there are hordes of storks in the fields. They walk about serenely looking for food. How I envy them. No one is pursuing them, no one is interested in where they came from, and where they are going, or whether they're Jewish or not. How I would like to be one of them now.

Although all sorts of thoughts are racing through my head, I don't forget for an instant that I must read every sign I see, so that I don't lose my way. At midday, when the sun is high in the sky I find a secluded place to eat my lunch. Within a jumble of high grass that hides me completely, I open the package that Esther prepared for me with great love, and eat it ravenously. Sitting in the grass in the summer serenity is very pleasant, but I don't remain there longer than it takes me to finish the sandwich. I must continue walking, because who knows what else will befall me today. I arrive at Zalucze late in the afternoon and after a short search I find the Bacher house.

The Bacher family is a mixed family. The father, Izy, is a Jew born in Jena, Germany. Since he was a Communist he fled to Poland when Hitler came into power. He is a dentist and a dental technician, but when starting out in Poland, he worked at various jobs. He painted artistic pictures on cloth and sold them, played the violin in an amateur orchestra. He was a house painter for a period of time, and had several other odd jobs. After a while he found a position in the city of Poznan working with a Jewish dentist, and that is where he met his future wife. The dentist had a servant, a young Polish girl called Irene, who did the cooking and cleaning in his clinic. When Izy arrived at the dentist's house, she helped him to adjust in Poland, since he didn't know one word of Polish. After a while they had a passionate romance and with time they had five children. Izy and Irene never got married and not all their children were baptized as Christians. The three older children were baptized mainly for economic reasons, rather than because of religious belief. The Church provides economic support for baptized children and the economic situation of the Bacher family at that time was very bad. The two younger children don't belong to any faith, not the Jewish faith and not the Christian. When the Germans were moving whole populations from place to place after the occupation, the Bacher family was moved to east Poland, as many Polish inhabitants were, while Germans living in east Poland were moved close to the German border, and even to Poznan.

When I arrive at the Bacher home, the father is no longer at there. Since the massacre in Wereszczyn, he has been hiding in the home of friends of the family in the neighboring village. I enter the Bacher house with a pounding heart. I am an uninvited guest and I don't know if they will accept me. I stand at the entrance to the house and suddenly I burst into uncontrollable crying and am unable to speak. With great difficulty I manage to get several words out of my mouth and to say who I am and why I came. Irene, mother of the family, greets me warmly. She recognizes me quickly and gives me the feeling that I've arrived at a safe harbor. She allows me to stay in their home and promises to treat me as though I were one of her own. My mother had been her husband's patient when he was still working, and Irene was acquainted with her and with us, the children. She also tells me that her husband had great respect for my father, and that they sometimes had heart to heart talks. She tries to calm me down and to make me feel that I am not a stranger to her. The first and important things that Irene says to me are, "Remember! Your parents were killed on the 14th of May, on a Wednesday, exactly the same day that my oldest son, Yoel, was born. All through our birthday celebrations we saw the smoke of burning Wereszczyn". Thanks to Irene, I am among the few survivors that know the exact day their family was annihilated. I have an exact *"Yahrzeit"* (the date to light a memorial candle).

In the Bacher family my first name remains Marisia and my family name becomes Bacher. My original name has gone underground until better days, if I manage to survive at all. Irene tells the neighbors that I am the daughter of relatives and was sent to help them temporarily because of economic difficulties. Mrs. Bacher accepts me warmly, however, everything is sparse in her household. I feel very ill at ease, because I quickly discover that the family is in great economic distress. Since the Bacher father is in hiding, there is no one to support the family. The only source of income remaining to them is selling the belongings from their former home in Poznan. There is little food – and now there is also one more mouth to feed – but no one in the family ever mentions that fact. I want to help in some way to pay for my own keep, but I don't know how. Suddenly I remember the secret basement in our house in Wereszczyn where there are still good clothes cloth, and valuables, which could be of great use and relieve the distress of the family here, if only we could somehow get to them. I tell Mrs. Bacher about this and suggest that we go to Wereszczyn and try to take the treasure from there. The kindness of the Postmaster towards me gives me courage and I hope that he won't cause difficulties about our taking the property hidden in our house, which is now being used as the post-office of the village. Irene takes my suggestion very seriously. She is aware that if we succeed the situation in her home will improve and her children won't suffer from hunger. She hires a horse and wagon and one morning, when it is still dark outside, she wakes me and tells me that we are going to Wereszczyn. I am very excited. This journey is very dangerous for me and for Irene. I'm afraid that if the farmers notice me, they're liable to report me and Irene to the Germans. But there is also a great temptation in this for me. I want to see my house again even if it's just once. Irene is the driver. She hurries the poor horse on with continued lashes of her whip. She is nervous and afraid and wants to reach our destination as quickly as possible. We arrive in the village very early, the farmers are not yet outside and they don't see us. We knock on the door, and I forget myself for a minute. Not so long ago this was my home, I wasn't in need of anyone's permission to enter it. Why must I now request permission to enter?

The sleepy Postmaster opens the door and is surprised to see me standing there with a strange woman. He let's us in and asks why we have come. I tell him about the secret basement and about the belongings kept there, and tell him that we have come to take them if he agrees. I look around me and am shocked by the terrible changes that have taken place. The large buffet standing on the entrance to the basement is the only thing that hasn't been moved. All the moveable things that were in the house have disappeared. The house looks deserted and orphaned, as though it's grieving for its dead inhabitants. The odors of our family are still emanating from the walls, the oven and the stove; the odor of mama's and grandma's cooking, of their baking and the scent of the sweat of my dear ones. A wave of longing engulfs me. The smells of my family are still so alive, while they, themselves, are rotting in the earth. If it were possible to preserve odors, they would be the first things I would take with me. I want them, I want to these smells to stay with them and I forget myself completely. The postmaster's voice brings me back to reality. He doesn't object to our taking the things from the basement, but requests that we do it quickly, before the villagers see us. In order to get to the basement we have to move the heavy buffet. We need help, and the postmaster kindly offers his. We open the lid of the basement and find the treasure there. We take out very many things. The wagon is filled with materials, my parents' furs, my mother's festive dresses, Passover dishes and many other things that were hidden from thieves. Everything I touch brings back a memory, which is now only mine and I have no one to share it with. The postmaster doesn't agree to take anything for himself, although we offer him anything he wants. He only requests that we leave something for the new neighbors living in the other half of the house so that they won't report him or us.

We leave Wereszczyn with our full wagon and I return to my shell with my memories and the pain of my loss. We arrive in Zalucze and Irene is very happy and proud of herself for succeeding in her mission. Her children are also happy with our success. They know that now their lives will be easier. Irene immediately begins to sell cloth to the villagers and it is literally snatched up. Such quality material isn't available now – even for money. The house is full of food and everyone is very pleased. With some of the cloth Irene sews new clothes for her children, and that also makes them happy. She widens my mother's dresses and wears them herself. It's difficult for me to see her in those clothes. They bring back sweet memories of my home, which doesn't exist anymore. It is very painful, but I keep the pain hidden deep in my heart. There is a feeling of wellbeing in the house and everyone is in a better mood. However, the well being is only temporary, until the goods are all sold. I feel much more at ease now, because I feel that my presence isn't a financial burden on the family. On the contrary, it has given them great relief.

The postmaster, a rare person, finds a package of family photographs in one of the closets of the house. In his great sensitivity, he understands that the package would be priceless for me. Despite his being in charge of the post office, he doesn't feel he can rely on its services, and decides to bring me the photographs himself. One day he arrives at Irene Zalucza's house and asks to see me. When we meet he puts the package of photos in my hand and says, "I know that this is the only thing left to you as a remembrance of your family. I kept them for you. It's the least I can do for you". I am very moved by his act and I don't know how to thank him. I will never forget that humane gesture. Thanks to the nobility of soul of the postmaster, my children and grandchildren recognize the faces of their uncles – my little brothers, and of their grandparents – my parents who were only twenty-eight years old when they were murdered.

A Singing Potato Peeler

My presence in Zalucze becomes problematic. Our Polish neighbors begin to suspect that I am Jewish and harass Irene and her children with all sorts of questions and threats. The Bacher family is suspect even without my presence, since everyone in the village knows that the father of the family is a Jew. The children are considered half-Jews, and can easily be accused of being impure Aryans. If the Germans discover that they're cross-breeds they may send them to a concentration camp, or kill them on the spot, in accordance with the Race Purity Law. Winter is on the way and another shelter must be found for the father of the family, who is presently hidden in the hayloft of a friend. The situation is complex and demands finding some creative solution, which will insure the safety of the entire family. They must re-organize their lives including where they live. Since my presence arouses suspicions, I am the first to be sent to another place. In Grabnik, the neighboring village, there is an estate, which previously belonged to an aristocratic Polish family and was appropriated by the German army. Germans are now living there. All the services there are based on the forced-labor of Jews and Poles. Among the Jewish laborers is the Zalc family from Poznan, which was friendly with the Bacher family even before the war. Irene brings me to this estate, to the Zalc family who are willing to take me temporarily. Again I am alone, in a new place, with strangers, and I must, once again, summon all my strength in order to adjust to life here. Shortly after my arrival I am added to the kitchen staff as a potato peeler in order to pay for my keep and to keep me occupied. During the cold autumn days in Poland, the kitchen is considered a good work place. The cold isn't as fierce as in the work places outside, and sometimes there is even some additional food.

There are six people in the Zalc family: the two parents, three boys – Abraham, Nathan and Alek, and one daughter called Roza. When I arrive, Abraham, the first-born is no longer alive. German soldiers, who live in the estate, killed him for the fun of it when they were boating in the nearby lake. They used him as a target in their target practice. Abraham had two duties. He was invited to play the accordion during the boating trip and also to serve as a live target. I am welcomed warmly by the Zalc family and develop a deep friendship with Roza, the daughter – a friendship that lasts for a very long time. Roza is ten years older than I am and acts as a mentor for me, like an older sister, and to a certain extent, a substitute mother. I am very attached to her, and love her unreservedly for many years afterward. Roza treats me like a little sister and tries to relieve my loneliness. There are no other children my age in the estate and she entertains me after work. The landscape around the estate in Grabnik is enchanting and we take many walks. There is a large lake and many water birds come there to find food. I look at those birds curiously and with envy. I would like to fly like them. Sometimes, when a Polish acquaintance from among the estate workers goes out to sail on the lake, we are invited to come along. Despite the fact that I'm a little afraid of the water, I enjoy it very much. There are four Polish girls among the potato peelers, members of the Krole family, who like me very much because of my singing talent. We all sing together a great deal while we're working, and they are so enamored with my voice that they invite me to come live with them. They want to have the pleasure of hearing me sing even after work hours. The Krole girls take me to all kinds of outings with their friends so that I can sing for them there. They refer to me as: "Our Nightingale".

In the winter, it's customary for the farmers to conduct evenings of plucking duck and goose feathers for filling their winter quilts and pillows. These evenings are accompanied by sing-along, solo singing and special foods. The girls take me with them to these evenings and are proud presenting me to their friends. The evenings are called "*Pjerzak*" in Polish and I remember them fondly. On these occasions I learned many Polish folk songs, and my singing was greatly admired, something that made me very proud.

The Zalc family encourages me to accept the Krole girls' offer to live with them. I have a better chance of survival there in the event of a sudden round-up of Jews. Although it's pleasant for me to live with the Zalc family, I move into the Krole home, because of the claim that I'll be safer there. The house is very crowded and there is no separate bed for me. I sleep with a different daughter each night. The beds are very small and they barely have enough room for one person. I take turns among the girls, in order not to be too much of a burden for any one of them. My life in Grabnik becomes routine. I have a roof over my head, I have work, and I also have an admiring young audience, whose company is very pleasant. For a while I become the 'little singing potato peeler', the darling of the Krole girls. My new status is very pleasing and gives me a sense of security. I stay in Grabnik for a number of months and I feel good there.

While I'm at the estate I have no idea that I will be returning to the Bacher family. None of them come to visit me, and no one tells me where I'm destined to be afterwards. I understand that I will not have a permanent home as I once had, and I think that my current home is the Grabnik Estate. One day without any previous warning, Irene appears and instructs me to pack my few belongings and return home with her. I am very surprised. Ever since the murder of my family, I've spent more time at Grabnik than with the Bacher family. I'm accustomed to the people and to the place. I enjoy the affection I've won here. I have no desire to leave, but I have no choice. Irene had brought me to the estate and she also has the right to take me back. I understand then that I essentially belong to her. I part from my four admirers, the girls of the Krole family, from the Zalc family and from Roza whom I love so much. I part from Regina, the beautiful Jewess, whom I will talk about later on, and I return with Irene to the Bacher family with tears running down my cheeks.

Beautiful Regina

One of the Jewish workers in the estate is a Jewish girl called Regina, Roza's childhood friend. Regina's great beauty is known in the entire area. Regina has no one in the estate, and perhaps nowhere else in the world. The Zalc family becomes Regina's family. I remember myself being enchanted by this girl and employing various tactics to attract her attention. To me she is as beautiful as a princess in a fairy-tale. She works as a chambermaid in the estate, always dressed in a white apron, and a white coif on her head that looks like a queen's crown. She always has a pleasant fragrance, and she doesn't resemble us, the potato peelers, in any way. She is loveliness itself. Regina is obliged to be amiable to the Germans – her employers, and to fulfill their requests quickly. She spends her free time with the Zalc family, and there, she is always exhausted and sad. I sometimes want to play with her, but she doesn't have the energy or the patience for games. I don't understand why she is so charming and smiley in the presence of the Germans, and so different when she is with us, who love her.

A young Polish worker on the estate, named Tadek, falls in love with Regina. He courts her tirelessly, pursues her wherever she goes, and doesn't give her any peace. Tadek has fair hair and blue eyes, and is tall and handsome– the embodiment of every young girl's dream. For a long time Regina doesn't respond to his advances, but he is relentless and continues in his efforts until he gets her attention and she returns his love. In time they become a recognized couple. According to the adult Jews among us, Regina is the only one among us who has a chance of surviving, because she is the lover of a Pole. We all sincerely hope that it will be so, but fate had other plans. When the final annihilation of the Jews in the area begins, Tadek hides her in his lodgings. I don't know why – either because of the nationalist neighbors' threats, or because he became tired of the Jewess – Tadek delivers Regina to the Germans in April 1943. He brings her to the Cycow Polish Police Station and delivers her to the angel of death for ten kilograms of sugar and a hundred Zloty. The country people tell Irene about Regina's death and even claim that the Germans mocked Tadek for delivering into their hands a flower of such rare beauty. The Germans don't spare her life, in spite of her great beauty. A Jewess, however beautiful, still belongs to the despised race. Her fate will be just the same as all the others belonging to her people.

I shed many tears when I hear about the death of my idol. I don't know any identifying details about her besides her rare beauty, not even her family name. What I do know is that her bones are interned somewhere in the earth of the town Cycow. Sometimes I see her before me in my imagination, as though she is demanding of me not to forget her. If my tale should ever be read, the words I used here to describe her will serve as her epitaph, and Regina will not sink into oblivion with no reminder of her existence.

Zalisocze

When Irene, my patron, comes to the Grabnik Estate and takes me back, we don't return to her previous residence in Zalucze, but to a remote village called Zalisocze, her new home. Irene chose this village very carefully, because of its remoteness and distance from any other village and because it is sparsely populated. The distance between the houses is over a kilometer. The village is also far from any government institution, of either the Germans or the Polish collaborators. In addition, the Mukhtar appointed by the Germans to keep order in the village, lives a great distance from Irene's new house. The absence of Germans in the area reduces any immediate danger to us. The seclusion of Zalisocze is ideal. It is surrounded by many trees, and contains vast grain fields– making it a comparatively easy place to escape to, and find cover in which to hide.

The house that Irene rented is essentially a large hayloft and not a residence; a room with large stoves, and a gigantic oven for baking bread is attached to the hayloft. The floor is made of compressed clay, with several boards in the center of the room resembling a small stage. When I am brought there, these boards serve as a lid for a secret hideaway used by Mr. Bacher, who has returned home. A large table, standing on the boards, serves to camouflage the hideaway. I am shocked by how crowded the place is. It's essentially a small room, which can barely house two beds, one for all six children, and the second for the parents. Between the two beds and near the window, which is the only source of light, there is a multi-purpose table with two benches attached on either side. Mr. Bacher's dental chair is squeezed in near the stove. The chair is kept for the dentist's use and also because of its value. There is no toilet either in the house or in the yard. When it isn't cold Irene and the children fertilize the fields around the house with their excrement.

For us who are imprisoned inside the house, there is a bucket. We have no choice but to use it in full view of everyone else. Each of us hates the bucket for reasons of his own. The children hate it because they have to empty it. I hate it because I can't get used to using it in the presence of other people. I always wait until I can't hold it in anymore and when I sit down on the bucket at the very last minute, smelly explosive noises are emitted and the children mock and tease me. They always have some comment and each time I feel humiliated anew. The smell from other members of the household doesn't engender any comments, only mine. I begin to feel that there is something wrong with me. Izy also uses the bucket and makes explosive noises and leaves a bad smell, but no one complains about it or makes hurtful remarks. The problem of moving my bowels becomes serious, but no one is aware of it and no one offers any help. For a while I try not to eat, but I can't hold out for long. I become so weak from this self-inflicted starvation that I don't have the strength to run to the bunker when necessary. No one guesses why I behave the way I do, why I suddenly stopped eating. Some members of the family think that this is my way of attracting attention. No one approaches me privately to find out what is really happening to me. Everyone is preoccupied with other issues.

When I came to the Bacher family in Zalucze I didn't have a hiding place. I walked about freely like the other children in the family. But in Zalisocze I was immediately hidden in the bunker that Izy, head of the family, uses as a hiding place. That was the first time I met him and after a while, when I knew him better, I learned to respect, admire and love him deeply. The hiding place is too small for both of us. It is urgent to build a new one, a real bunker. The new bunker is dug in the earth under the stove and the adjacent oven. The air opening is located where the ashes from the stove accumulate. The air coming in is very limited, and I develop an irreversible defect in my lungs. The hideout is small and humid and the clay earth constantly secretes drops of water. It is always completely dark inside, and the place is very depressing. Mr. Bacher has a special place where he can stand, but I only have a tiny corner where I can sit curled up. Sometimes, when I don't get into the bunker in time, they hide me in a bed with all the bedding piled on top of me and then I have even less air to breath than I have in the bunker. Lying hidden in bed is much more difficult than sitting in a dark bunker. I have to lie there without moving, my slightest movement is liable to attract the attention of a visitor. Irene's neighbors constantly suspect her of hiding Jews and we must be very cautious. When I lie there smothered by blankets, I am certain that the visitors are staring at the bed, and that thought paralyzes me. The hardest thing is when I feel I have to move my bowels. My bladder and my stomach don't understand my situation; they make their requirements known and I have to develop a special ability to withstand those demands. It's an excruciating punishment to lie still when there is pressure on the bladder or the intestines. Because of that suffering, I sometimes needlessly jump into the bunker, even when I just imagine that someone is approaching the house. After a while I learn to get into the bunker so quickly that I hardly ever have to hide in bed.

The bunker, which becomes our main home, is gradually improving. We expand it so that each of us has the possibility of standing and sitting and even more. I receive a large knife with a long blade and a straw basket. As I sit in the bunker I claw the moist clay wall and pull out chunks of clay, thus enlarging our living space. For every basketful of clay that I succeed in digging out with my knife, I receive a prize from father Bacher. He sometimes participates in enlarging the bunker, but I am generally the one who works at it. We spend most of the day deep in the ground and hardly ever see the sun. When the work of enlarging the bunker is done, the instruments that father Bacher used as a dentist are hidden next to him, just in case.

On my arrival to Zalisocze, I find that the Bacher family has severe economic problems again. The cloth and all the other valuables we brought back from our basement in Wereszczyn have been sold long ago. The family no longer has any valuables to sell and is suffering from hunger. We eat mainly potato peels that the children succeed in obtaining from the village farmers. Sometimes they succeed in stealing some beets and some turnips, but this is a rare festive event. Winter is at its height, and in addition to hunger, we are plagued by the terrible cold and there is no money to buy wood. Finding branches and roots in the snow and on the frozen ground is very difficult. The family is on the brink of despair. There doesn't seem to be any solution and dying of hunger or of the cold becomes a fearful possibility.

Black and White Lice

Despite the difficult conditions the family was living in, they don't know what lice are until I come to live with them. Irene is obsessive about the cleanliness of her children. Once a week, there is a permanent ceremony of bathing the whole gang in a round wooden tub generally used for laundry. The heads and bodies of each child are duly scrubbed and fortunately for them, they have no idea what lice look like and how it feels when you have them. I refuse to bathe because it's done publicly in the one room we all live in. I'm bashful about undressing before the children and am also afraid that they'll discover that I have lice. The lice, however, don't remain just with me. The six of us sleep together in the same bed, and the lice crawl to my neighbors to the right and to the left of me, to the Bacher children. Their heads and bodies begin to itch, but each time I am asked if I feel itchy, I claim that I don't, and that I don't feel anything unusual.

Irene and her husband evidently realize where the lice come from, but they don't want to pressure me so soon after my arrival. Three weeks later they begin to examine me. Actually, my clothes are so full of lice they could walk away on their own. My head is in similar condition. The moment I take my clothes off and Irene sees how full of lice they are she immediately throws them into the flaming stove. I am completely naked and am immersed into the round wooden tub for a basic scrubbing. All five children watch the show with great curiosity and a bit of pleasure. Until now they have never seen me nude and they scrutinize me thoroughly. Irene publicly points out all the defects she finds in my body. To this day I don't understand why she did that and with what intention. She declares that I have a crooked back and perhaps I'll develop a humpback if I don't get the proper treatment after the war. She shows everyone that I'm pigeon-toed and have flat feet, words that I don't even understand, but I understand that they point to some kind of defect. I am too skinny; my feet are big and wide and don't look feminine; My eyebrows aren't full enough and my lashes are too small, and other defects I hadn't been aware of. This public assessment of my defects shames and humiliates me deeply. At that moment I would have liked to vanish.

I have two thick braids that my mother tended lovingly for many years. She washed them, combed them, wound colorful ribbons into them and took great pride in them. These braids are very precious to me. They are the last reminder of my mother's loving touch. My braids are also full of lice. The lice in my clothes are almost white and it's difficult to detect them. The lice in my hair are darker, closer to the color of my hair and they're smaller than those in my clothes. They are well camouflaged and almost impossible to see. In addition they lay many little white eggs that stick to the hair and are very difficult to get rid of. The lice irritate me no end. I despise them and I despise myself when they crawl all over me. Since my mother was killed my hair hasn't ever been washed or combed properly.

Irene now decides to correct that condition and to get rid of the lice. She decides that the best way to accomplish this mission is to cut off my braids. Within me I strongly object to parting from my precious braids, but I'm afraid to outwardly oppose Irene's decrees. In my heart I believe there are other ways to accomplish the same objective, if one really wants to. I had heard of using kerosene and a thick-toothed comb, but I don't dare suggest those things to Irene. The treatment demands time and patience, and Irene doesn't have a surplus of either one of these where I'm concerned. Since I can't carry out that treatment myself, I'm obliged to keep quiet. Irene appoints Izy to carry out the project, and he, without any warning, takes a large pair of scissors, cuts my braids off one at a time and throws them directly into the fire. I feel even more orphaned. The last vestige of my lost home and my previous life is taken from me. After the cutting of my braids, my head is shaved in order to insure the complete destruction of the lice eggs and to free the family of the plague. The memory of the pain and sadness I kept locked inside me when my braids went up in smoke is still with me to this day. I have the feeling that my mother mourns for them with me. I feel terrible without my hair and with a shaven head. I feel that I look like an ugly, repulsive scarecrow and not at all like a girl. The mirror reflects back to me the face of an ugly boy with gigantic ears and bulging eyes. All my girlish charm has disappeared. I think that if my mother were to rise from her grave and look at me, she wouldn't recognize me as her beloved daughter. I wasn't allowed to let my hair grow back even a little until the end of the war. Every few weeks I was shaved again. I carry the complex of my shaven head with me even today as a grandmother. After the war I tried again and again to grow braids, but with no success.

Greater than all the Blacksmiths

One cold snowy evening when we are cuddled around the barely heated stove, someone knocks loudly on the door. The arrival of a stranger on such a cold evening is very unusual and we dash to the bunker in alarm. The whole family is afraid of a surprise search and the children cuddle together on the bench near the stove, which is above the entrance to the bunker. Irene goes to see who is at the door – but not before she is certain that we are already inside the bunker. She is greatly surprised to discover that the person standing behind the door is a farmer begging her to let him in and rescue him. "I have a terrible tooth-ache and no blacksmith in the village is prepared to extract the tooth because of its strange shape". He heard that she's a dentist's wife and pleads with her, even demands of her to extract the accursed tooth causing him so much pain. Irene knows nothing about dentistry, and has never even worked as a dental assistant. Her only experience in the field is when she helped her children to pull out their loose baby teeth. Pulling out the big, strangely shaped tooth of a grown man is beyond her abilities. She doesn't tell the man that she has no experience in dentistry; she just apologizes for not having the proper instruments.

The farmer doesn't relent, he informs her that he's not moving from her house with that aching tooth and that she is his last resort; he's suffering terribly and she must help him before he goes out of his mind. Izy hears this conversation from the bunker and since all his instruments are in the bunker beside him, he decides he has nothing to lose and chooses suitable pliers. He puts them through the bunker opening, which is close to where the children are sitting and touches his son's leg with them. He whispers to his son to give the pliers to Irene, who will know what to do with them. His son, Yoel, pretends to be looking for something in the silverware cupboard and tells Irene that he's found pliers among the spoons and forks. Irene immediately understands and takes the pliers, deciding to make an attempt to extract the tooth. The worst thing that can happen is that she will fail, like the blacksmiths of the area, however if she succeeds, it will be a great achievement for her. She sits the farmer down on the dentist chair, and with one powerful wrench she extracts the terrible tooth. In spite of the pain, the blood and the puss flowing from his mouth, the farmer doesn't complain, he is happy that he finally found someone to put an end to his suffering. He rinses his mouth with the water Irene serves him. Then he gets down on his knees in a theatrical gesture, taking off his hat to this heroic woman who succeeded in doing what no blacksmith in the area dared to try.

The farmer showers her with thanks from the bottom of his heart. He heaps praise and compliments on her and in the end, asks her how he can repay her. Irene is in desperate need of money but she has no idea what price to ask for extraction. She says to the farmer, "My children haven't had a full meal for weeks, give me a sum that can buy at least enough bread for one week". I remember that the farmer gave her forty zloty. I don't know if that's a small or a large sum, but it became the permanent price we always charged for the extraction of a tooth. I also remember that the next day we sated ourselves on fresh bread, a real celebration for us. Irene's success in doing something that no blacksmith dared to do spread as quickly as lightning in the whole area. I don't think that the modern means of communication would spread the news as quickly as it was spread among the farmers. The greatest admiration came from the men.

Izy Bacher's brilliant idea – to try to accomplish the nearly impossible – in order to save his family from starvation, turned into a great economic success. Fortunately for us, despite the fact that the first tooth extraction was carried out without sterilization of the instruments used, the farmer didn't suffer any complications as a result. We were now able to alleviate our hunger. The Bacher couple began to make plans for opening a dental clinic in order to overcome our economic difficulties.

An Invisible Dentist

Irene becomes more and more famous as a courageous dentist. Farmers come not just for tooth extractions, but also for other treatments like fillings, crowns and even false teeth. The Bacher couple who have a large family to support, and who didn't do well financially even before the war, is now considering opening a dental clinic in their house. Irene has never studied dentistry, but Izy is both a dentist and a dental technician and can expertly guide her in both branches of the profession. They're planning a system where Izy would be a secret and invisible advisor, and Irene would carry out his instructions.

Izy finds a place near the air inlet of the bunker to set up a magnifying mirror, which enables him to see inside the customer's mouth. The dental chair is placed opposite the stove, at an angle suitable for Izy to see inside the patient's mouth. Izy also hears the patient's complaints from the bunker. After the patient leaves, Izy explains to Irene how to treat his teeth when he comes again. When a new customer comes, Irene places some cotton soaked in disinfectant into his mouth. This makes an impression on most of the farmers because of the sharp smell of the disinfectant. This process of sterilization enables the Bachers to survey the patient's mouth and the condition of his teeth. The survey also gives Irene time to learn from Izy what kind of treatment to use in the next visit. In preparation for the subsequent visits, Izy lays out the needed instruments and teaches Irene how to use them. Although Irene receives instructions from her husband, the work that she does demands great effort and daring. At the time I didn't see anything out of the ordinary in what Irene was doing, but when I matured I understood how difficult it was for her. Many of the Bachers' actions at that time were deceitful and wouldn't be considered legitimate in a normal situation. However, the struggle for survival during the war legitimizes many strange and dubious actions. I don't believe that I or anyone else would be capable of becoming a dentist over-night, if I hadn't witnessed that first extraction and all the other dental treatments Irene carried out. And if someone were to tell me the story, I would think it was a fabrication.

The Bacher family is in possession of dental tools and instruments, but they don't have the materials needed for regular work. The whole idea of opening a dental clinic is worthwhile only if they find a way of obtaining those materials. They will not be able to support the family, for any length of time, just on extractions. In a playful mood they calculate that they would have to extract the teeth of all the farmers in the area in order to make a decent living. Hunger is still a real threat to the family and they must find a solution. The Bachers spend several days and nights debating what to do. Irene can't go to Lublin, the nearest big city, to buy the needed substances because it would take her several days and it's too dangerous to leave us alone. She has no friends that she could send in her stead. The situation seems hopeless. In the end, after much indecision, Irene and Izy decide to take the risk and order the materials by mail just as they used to do before Izy went into hiding. They hope that the Germans won't inquire as to the ancestry of the person making the order. They aren't certain that the same shop still exists and functions, but they must try. The order is sent in the same way it had been sent in the past and the family starts a period of waiting. When the cherished package with the ordered materials finally arrives, the opening of the clinic becomes a reality. We are on the threshold of solving the problem of our economic survival.

Smelting Gold

Once extracting teeth, filling cavities and other dental treatments become habitual, the Bacher family decides to go a step further. Izy, who is knowledgeable in all the technical work required for the preparation of crowns and false teeth, decides to add those to his services. There's no danger involved in this because it doesn't require personal contact with the patient, while it does create the possibility of increasing their income. Irene will receive remote control lessons from Izy in this field as well, and she is ready to take her chances, considering all her previous successes.

One of the first orders is for a golden crown from a young girl who wishes to impress the object of her admiration. The crown is meant to raise her status in the eyes of the young man. Irene tells the girl that if she wants a gold crown, she must bring a gold ring of high quality. She explains that the ring will be smelted and then forged into a crown the size suitable for her tooth.

Izy doesn't have any means of forging metals. Since one of the most common methods of forging is the use of intense and focused heat, Izy builds a bellows like that used by blacksmiths, in order to create a source of compressed air that will fan the flame. We children take turns jumping on the bellows in order to create a stream of air, which flows through a pipe to a burning flame. The oxygen in the air coming from the bellows raises the heat of the flame, which is aimed at a glob of metal, until the metal finally gives way and changes from solid to liquid. As soon as the problem of smelting is solved, the sky is the limit. Izy, who is an artisan with golden hands, shapes samples of crowns out of wax in the shape of the patient's tooth. He then pours plaster around the wax crown. When the plaster dries it is possible to pour the molten gold (or any other metal) into it, because the wax inside the plaster melts from the heat of the metal and is replaced by the liquid metal. Years later, when I was visiting a plant for producing spare parts for aircraft, I discovered that they employ a very similar method, (using wax and plaster), to the one I remember from the war days.

We do all the technical work at night. The only window in the house is covered on the inside by a heavy curtain so that Izy's shadow can't be seen outside. I am one of Izy's most devoted and available helpers in all the technical work. I jump on the bellows, mix the plaster with water and make a dough-like mixture, into which we place the wax form. Actually I help with all the things that a child my age can do. Since I'm imprisoned within the house and can't play or do the things children my age do, I'm happy to spend my time helping Izy. I gradually accumulate knowledge and experience, which are very useful in the technical work and personally gratifying for me. The transition to making false teeth and crowns greatly improves the economic situation of the family, which eventually becomes even better than it was before the war. There is plenty of food and more money than is needed for our daily upkeep. Irene decides to use the surplus money for buying various things, to prepare for the days after the war.

Remnants of the Zalc Family

The Zalc family, with whom I lived at the Grabnik Estate, led a relatively peaceful life until the end of 1942. When the final extermination of the Jews in the area began, the Zalc family decides to find a hiding place where they can live while the Jews are being taken to concentration camps– and perhaps to survive until the end of the war. They have many Polish friends at the estate, from whom they try to get help from in time of need. The Germans killed the two oldest sons, Abraham and Nathan, beforehand. The rest of the family; father, mother, daughter and little son put up a tent in a richly vegetated, marsh area, where they plan to live until the danger passes. Since the family is now well to do, they contact two young Polish workers from the Estate, (who are considered friends of the family), and request that they supply the family with food in exchange for money. The young men are meant to sell different articles belonging to the Zalc family, to take a good percent of the selling price for themselves, and to use the rest of the money to buy food for the family. This arrangement works well for several months. The Zalc family feels relatively secure, because only these two young Poles know where they are, and both of them have been close family friends for a long time. It doesn't occur to anyone to suspect the boys of any possible deceit. One day the boys are given expensive, elegant fur collars to sell. Furs like that are very rare in our neighborhood and are considered precious treasures. They should bring in enough food to feed the family when the snow makes it impossible to reach the tent. The boys are expected to return with the food within the next two days – as they usually do. When more than two days pass, and the boys don't make an appearance, Mr. Zalc decides to take the risk and go to the boys' lodgings to see what's causing the delay. The family's food supply is dwindling and they face the danger of starving. The remaining three members of the family are left waiting anxiously for his return, and when time passes and he doesn't return, the two children, Roza and Alek decide to look for him. Since they suspect that the two Polish boys have betrayed them, they advance cautiously in the dark in the direction of the boys' lodging.

Suddenly they hear groans in the shrubbery. They approach the place and find their father lying there, bleeding profusely, his skull crushed, but still alive. They begin to drag him away in the hope of somehow saving him. After a while, Alek and Roza see blinking lights from two flashlights approaching them. It is clear from the movements of the flashlights that they are being used to urgently look for something. The two Polish friends of the family are searching for their victim. They are bigger and stronger than the two children dragging their wounded father. The children must decide quickly whether to continue dragging their father, who has no chance of survival, or to leave him there and save themselves and their mother, who is waiting in the tent. They decide to leave their father, whose chances for staying alive are slight. The choice is very hard for them, but gives them the chance to survive. Roza and Alek run as fast as they can to the tent. They take their mother, who has been anxiously waiting for them, out of the tent, leave all their possessions there and hide in the reeds growing in the lake nearby. The two Polish boys arrive, looking for the other members of the family, in order to kill them and take whatever possessions are left. Despite their thorough search inside and around the tent, they don't succeed in finding the inhabitants. It doesn't occur to them that their victims are sitting in the freezing water of the lake. It seems impossible to them. When they give up their search, they take the tent with everything in it and leave. The remnants of the Zalc family get out of the lake and begin to walk in the direction of Zalisocze where the Bacher family live.

We hear knocking at the window with the first light of dawn. Izy and I dash into the bunker, fearing that our Polish neighbors are coming again to search the house. Irene peeks through the window and on discovering who it is, opens the door for them, but doesn't reveal that her husband and I are hiding in the bunker. She sets out food for the Zalc family, dries their clothes, and temporarily hides them in the hayloft attached to the house, until she can think of a more permanent solution. The Bacher family is unsure how to deal with the situation. Mother Zalc has one lame leg and is very limited in her mobility. If they take her in she is liable to endanger us all. Irene agrees to take the son and daughter and plans to find shelter for the mother somewhere else. Irene tells Mother Zalc that she has found a refuge for the two children, but she doesn't tell her where. Irene suggests she say goodbye to them and promises her to find shelter for her within a few days.

Seventeen year old Alek, who is the only man left in the family, doesn't agree to leave his mother alone and decides to remain with her. The mother and Alek suggest that only Roza go to the hiding place that Irene has found for her. Roza parts from her mother and brother and Irene hides her in our bunker where she sits on the other side of the wall from where her family is – without either of them knowing it. For reasons of security, Roza is separated from her family by a wall for an entire week without the possibility of seeing one another. I, who yearn for my own mother, can't understand how she is able to bear it. At the end of the week Irene takes her mother and brother to a hideaway at a farmhouse, and Roza doesn't ever see them again.

I don't know any details about the hardships that Alek and his mother encountered afterwards. However, I do know that they eventually reached Ghetto Wlodawa. They were caught when the ghetto was eradicated and died in the extermination camp, Sobibor. In the course of the years Roza, who was ten years older than I, became the person I felt closest to in all the world and the wells of love that lay dormant inside me for such a long time were secretly showered upon her.

Our Malicious Neighbors

Despite the fact that most of the villagers from near and far are in need of Irene's services, the people in our village lay in wait for her all the time. They are avowed Jew-haters and keep a close watch over everything that goes on in our house. Katorski and his sons, our next-door neighbors, who are extreme nationalists, keep a permanent watch under our window at night. They want to know if there are suspicious voices in the house. They would especially like to know if a man's voice can be heard, because they always suspect that Irene is hiding a Jewish husband. That's the reason that Mr. Bacher has been speaking in a whisper for two years. The children don't call him "Papa", but use the word "you" as they do with everyone else. Roza and I are not called by our names, but by pet names. I'm called Bunny, which in Polish has the connotation of being weak and cowardly. I hate that name. I don't feel that my behavior is cowardly. It's not my fault that I'm obliged to rush into the bunker every time someone approaches the house. For me it's a matter of survival, and I find the image very insulting. I don't remember Roza's pet name, but I'm certain it wasn't in any way hurtful.

Katorski and his Jew-hating friends are not content with eavesdropping outside our house; they also take the law into their own hands and conduct periodic surprise searches in our living quarters. Their first search is conducted shortly after I arrive from the Grabnik Estate to Zalucze. On a freezing winter night they break into the house with axes in their hands and uproot the seven boards that cover the floor in the center of the room. They are sure there is a hiding place under the boards where Jews are hiding. Fortunately for us, this time they don't look in any other parts of the room. At the time our hideout was moved under the stove, which is evidently not a conceivable place for a hideout in their eyes. They leave furiously empty handed.

The second search takes place a year later and it almost costs us our lives. Again, in the middle of the night, there is a loud knock on the door. The three of us barely make it into the bunker. And they are already in the house, armed with pickaxes and gigantic blacksmith hammers. They begin to bang on the wall in back of the stove, and shatter one brick after another in order to reach the hideout. They have evidently overheard in their eavesdropping sessions, which are also held in the hayloft, that something is going on underground in the area of the stove. Fortunately for us, it doesn't occur to them that the entrance to the bunker is located on the other side of the stove, where the fire is lit. They knock furiously on the walls of the stove and find only bricks. The sound of the pickaxes comes closer and closer to us. My heart is pounding so hard with fear, that it seems to me it can be heard outside. I am convinced that this is the end. I again repeat the prayer that is said before death over and over–

"Hear, O Israel" – and my whole body is shivering. Each one of us is dealing with his fear in his own way – and that fear, is the fear of death. Even Izy, who always manages to look calm and restrained, doesn't succeed in hiding his fear this time.

The Germans have instilled into the Poles the understanding that there are no limits to what one may do in order to find and report hidden Jews. We know that those anti-Semites will stop at nothing to rid the village of every remaining Jew. We are helpless. Irene and the children outside are as frightened as we are. They are just hoping that the malicious neighbors won't think of searching on the other side of the stove. With vicious threats and shouts, our neighbors take apart the gigantic stove bit by bit and on finding nothing they angrily leave the house empty-handed. As they leave they threaten Irene that if she ever dares to help Jews, she and her children will pay for it dearly.

After that search the Bacher family makes two major decisions. First, they must quickly dig a new hiding place, because the current one has become suspect and second, Irene must obtain the Mukhtar's defense against such surprise searches initiated privately by residents of the village. After a short while they make another important decision, to obtain a gun at any price, in order not to be left defenseless against murderous Jew haters.

A New Hiding Place

Several days after the night search that our neighbors conduct at our house, Irene decides to go to the Police Station in Cycow in order to invite the senior officers to the home of the Mukhtar of the village. She wants to prepare a welcoming, in part, as an opportunity to tell them of the searches made in her house on the initiative of Polish residents of the village. She wants to request that German government representatives conduct a search in her house themselves to see if she is hiding any Jews. She wants to be rid, once and for all, of these surprise searches conducted by law-breaking villagers, who place themselves above the German government and do whatever they please in the home of a lone woman without a husband. Inviting the Germans to search her house is a clever ploy, but a dangerous one. On the day of Irene's journey our house is closed to visitors. The children are instructed as to what to answer people who come for dental treatment, as well as to others just visiting. In the meanwhile the three of us start digging a new hole in the earthen floor under the bed. The earth dug up for the new hideout fills in the former bunker under the oven. We must work quickly, but carefully. Irene might come with the Germans before we are ready. It was agreed with Irene that she would delay her arrival with the Germans as much as possible. In the meantime she gives the Mukhtar a generous amount of money to prepare a festive meal with alcoholic drinks for him and for the Germans. Afterwards she travels to the police station in Cycow to bring the guests to the feast she is organizing. Amongst other things they will be expected to conduct the search in our house.

In the meanwhile we work without interruption, digging a niche in the clay floor under the bed, which is just barely enough for crowded seating for three people. In the early evening the new hideaway is more or less ready. Fatigued from the work and the tension, we enter the new pit that we dug and pray that the search won't take too long. We sit crouched together in an almost impossible position and we won't be able to hold out under those conditions for any length of time. Izy dug a small air hole for us in the direction of the rabbit burrow, adjacent to the wall of the house just above our new hiding place. It's difficult to bear the smell of urine and rabbit excretion that fills our niche. However, there is an advantage. If the Germans bring tracking dogs with them the pungent smell will confuse them and they won't be able to smell us. We sit in the new hideout for several hours, waiting for the Germans that Irene is supposed to bring for a search. The old hideout is piled with the earth from the new hideout and the old opening is also stopped up and white washed. The stove is burning full force to dry it out as quickly as possible. The three of us are sitting with folded limbs, squeezed together, and almost suffocated by the odor of the rabbits.

At midnight, when we are faint with fear and the lack of air, paralyzed and feeling pain in every limb, Irene returns home. She comes alone, without the Germans and without the Mukhtar. We are allowed to leave the foul smelling hideout and enter the house. I can't move my legs or my other limbs. Izy and Roza are in similar condition. We have something to eat and drink, because over the course of this entire crazy day, not one thing entered our mouths. Irene is fatigued from her hard day, but she is very pleased. She tells us, and her children, who were no less frightened than we were on that day, about her adventures. It turns out that she succeeded in gathering a delegation of police officers from the police station in Cycow, and brought them to the home of the Mukhtar in Zalucze. They were all treated to a festive meal with much to drink. Irene, who speaks German fluently, was a most charming hostess. At the end of the meal when most of the guests were already inebriated, she demanded of the police officers to come home with her and conduct a proper search in her house. "She wants, once and for all", she tells them, "to prove that she is not hiding any dirty Jews in her house". Both the police, and the Mukhtar, refuse to comply with this request. Irene insists. She is really adamant so that her performance will be all the more convincing. When they are resolute in their refusal, Irene demands a signed document, written in black and white, stating that only the Germans, (and perhaps their official allies), will be allowed to conduct searches in her house, and not just any Polish farmer who decides to take the law into his own hands. In the event that one of her Polish neighbors harasses her, she will turn directly to the German Police to protect her. Irene had succeeded in receiving the document she requested from the Germans and she made certain that all her dental patients know of its existence in order to frighten her neighbors. From then on the surprise searches ceased, but the eavesdropping continued.

The Revolver

Purchasing weapons during the German occupation is complicated and dangerous, but not impossible. It is forbidden for a Pole to carry arms. If a Pole is caught with a weapon in his possession the punishment is death. In such circumstances, one needs a great deal of money, utter secrecy and complete mutual trust between the buyer and the seller in order to obtain weapons. Irene and Izy found it hard to decide which one of their dental patients they could rely on to purchase a revolver for them. After a thorough appraisal of all their patients, they approach a woman who makes the impression that she is well educated, openly anti-Nazi, and who doesn't express any anti-Semitic sentiments, as so many of our patients do. Irene explains her need to purchase a weapon by telling her that she is a woman living alone, without a man in the house, and is often harassed by the villagers. She explains to her patient that the revolver is meant only for self-defense, and promises her that the transaction will be made in utmost secrecy. The woman understands Irene's need for a weapon and promises to make every effort to help her. After a comparatively short while the awaited revolver arrives. The price is unbelievably high, but the sense of security it grants all of us is impossible to measure in money. I will never forget the moment that the revolver arrived. I, who felt like a hunted animal, easy prey for any predator, suddenly feel completely different. I now have a means of defense at my disposal, which gives me a sense of self-respect, and the ability to choose an honorable death if, God forbid, there is no choice.

At the age of ten I learn how to use a revolver. I still remember how to load it, how the cylinder, which is perforated with six openings, gets filled with bullets, how to lock the gun and release the lock – and also how to shoot. We agree that if hostile people discover us and wish us harm or intend to report us to the Germans, we won't surrender easily. We'll either fight for our lives or commit suicide. The revolver is placed in a special recess in the wall of our hideout, next to Izy. It is loaded and ready for use when needed. Fortunately for us, we were never in a situation where we needed it. I can't imagine what would have happened to us if we ever really had to use it. Looking back, I'm amazed by our naivety. What could we actually have done with six bullets? What would happen to the family if we had tried to fight? But at the time, having the gun made us feel secure. While the gun was in our possession, I often imagined myself resisting those who came to attack us and even succeeded in defeating them. None of my imaginary battles convince the Bacher children that I'm not a frightened little rabbit, but a heroic girl who succeeds in defeating all our enemies with the aid of one revolver.

Tensions and Irritations

Our house in Zalisocze, as mentioned above, has only one room. The crowded conditions and the constant contact with one another create permanent tensions, especially between the children and me. There are many arguments amongst the Bacher children themselves and they often come to blows. For the children, I'm an outsider and my presence in their crowded house is very irritating. They think that I'm given special privileges because chores they are assigned to do aren't expected of me. This is an additional source of annoyance. I don't participate in emptying the pail used for our excrements, and it's difficult for them to accept this, despite the fact that they know that I mustn't be seen outside. The constant stench in the house irritates all of us and even though it also belongs to all of us, they mainly blame me. I don't help in gathering firewood and in carrying out other chores that they hate. They resent me and express it by making me their scapegoat. In addition they resent the guard duty they're assigned to everyday, a duty I am not expected to perform. They refuse to understand that I can't do guard duty as they do and they don't care about the reason. They see me as a shirker who sits in their home, receives everything and doesn't help with anything. They hate to gather firewood in the winter. They have to walk great distances in the snow and their feet get wet, because the heavy wooden soles of their shoes are not high enough to keep out the snow. The work itself is hard and the axe often misses the mark. I, of course, am sitting at home while they're freezing outside. I'm also not required to go on errands in the village. Many of these errands are very unpleasant and the fact that I'm not required to do them upsets the children no end. It doesn't occur to them that I would be prepared to run any errand and do every chore – if that meant I could go out into the fresh air as they do, instead of being imprisoned in a dark hole.

The house is meticulously guarded day and night, so that no unwelcome guests, who might report us to the German authorities, can take us by surprise. The day is divided into shifts and each child does two hours guard-duty. There is a cherry-tree right in front of the house, and in order not to attract attention and also to expand his field of vision; the guard is posted among the branches of the tree. From there he is hidden from sight and has a good observation point on the road leading to our house. When a figure is seen at a distance on the road, the guard climbs down the tree and announces that someone is coming in the direction of our house. We, the three Jews, quickly jump into the bunker and close the lid above us. Since we are never certain what the destination of the stranger really is, we take no chances; there are days that we jump into the bunker in vain, time after time, because of some innocent passer-by. My body is covered with black and blue marks from those frequent jumps. The entrance to the bunker is very small, making it easy to close, and I never jump through it without hurting myself even though I am the smallest of the three. Because of their size, Izy and Roza have many more black and blue marks than I do, but their blue marks don't hurt me, as I am focused only on my own pain.

Guard-duty is much more complicated in the winter. It's impossible to sit in the tree because of the cold and the lack of foliage, which completely exposes the guard. There is no other hiding place outside, making it necessary to invent different strategies to avoid arousing the suspicions of the neighbors or passers-by. On winter days that aren't particularly cold, the children do guard-duty outside the house, under the guise of playing games. Izy invents a device, which further improves the process. He builds an underground alarm bell, activated by a knock on the door. When a figure appears on the horizon, one of the guards throws a rock or knocks on the door, activating the bell, which signals us to jump into the bunker. Now guard-duty is easier and more efficient since it is unnecessary to enter the house to announce that someone is approaching.

As mentioned before, the children are very annoyed by the obligation to guard the house, and because of that, they envy me. The children are never as free as they would like to be, but they are not obligated to hide as I am. I, who, in any event don't do anything, am not obliged to guard. In their eyes this is unjust. They consider me lazy, sitting in the house and shirking chores that are assigned to them. They don't see my helping Izy, or the cooking and peeling of vegetables I do when I'm not in the bunker, as actual work. They see my exemption from guard-duty as an unforgivable privilege and a justification for persistently tormenting me. On especially severe winter days, when the snow is heavy and there's little chance that someone will venture going outside, I guard the house from inside. There is a peek hole in our padded, double door, from which it is possible to watch the road leading to our house, and I look out of that peek hole for many hours. If there are several consecutive days like that, I do guard duty all the time, but that doesn't satisfy the gang and doesn't reduce their anger. The Bacher children's annoyance and jealousy of me are fixed, and it doesn't matter what I do or what I don't do. Since they are occupied during the day and they have no possibility of hurting me physically in the presence of the adults, they take their revenge secretly, every night in our communal bed. On many nights I pray to God to murder me at night and bring me back to life in the morning. I no longer have the strength to withstand the daily persecution and torture that the Bacher children devise, but I say nothing and suffer in silence. I don't have anyone to complain to, and I know that if I were to object, the harassment would be doubled.

Feather Parties

The one-room apartment where nine people live has multiple functions. It serves as a living room, a dentist clinic, a dining room, a bedroom, a guest room and a workroom, all at the same time. In other words, it's used for everything. There are only two beds in the room, one for the parents and the other for the seven children from age nine to twenty after Roza joined us. There is just one feather quilt for the seven of us, which isn't big enough to sufficiently cover us all, especially those sleeping on the edges. Due to the bitter cold of the winter nights, those sleeping on the edge make desperate attempts to keep covered. The endless pulling in opposite directions sometimes tears the quilt and the feathers come out and fly all over the house. The surrealistic picture we make, covered in white feathers, greatly amuses one of the Bacher children and after a while he begins to deliberately tear the quilt. The one accused of tearing the quilt and of throwing the feathers about is, of course – me.

During the winter, there is a feather throwing party every night. Yakov is the champion tearer. He makes a big hole in the quilt, tosses the feathers with his foot, and announces in a loud voice, "The rabbit did it again, she tore the quilt again". Of course, he means me. The feathers fly around the house, covering everyone's head, the dental tools, the dishes, and everything else. We all work together to collect the feathers, to mend the quilt and put the house in order so that it can function normally in the morning. Everyone looks at me angrily, because the feather parties take up precious sleeping time, and I am blamed for that. At first, I really believe that I am the one who tears the quilt while sleeping. But I also notice that it doesn't matter where I sleep, in the middle or on the edge, the quilt is always torn during the night. Since changing my place doesn't help, I begin to stay awake at night, so that I won't tear the quilt. I'm angry with myself for keeping the whole family from sleeping. If I don't sleep at night, the quilt won't be torn, there won't be feather throwing and maybe I'll stop being the object of anger and blame. I stay awake for hours, and soon discover that I'm not to blame for the tears in the quilt. It's Yaakov, who is two years older than I am. He is the serial tearer who does it deliberately. I'm in a serious bind. If I squeal on Yaakov, the children will take heavy revenge. I no longer see any point in staying awake all night. What should I do? I'm fatigued from helplessness.

In my waking hours, my thoughts return time and time again to the mass grave in Wereszczyn and I try to imagine what is happening there. When strong winds wail outside, they sound to me like the crying of my dead family who are probably cold and wet and pleading for help. My heart goes out to them. Sometime I envy them. If the dead really don't feel anything, I would like to be a little bit dead in order not to suffer so much. I tell Roza about my problem, and she has no advice for me, and also no words of consolation. She hints that Irene encourages the children to harass me and to this day, I don't understand why. If Irene encourages the children to harass me, there is no chance that the children will ever leave me in peace. In the end, Clara, the eldest of the Bacher children, feels sorry for me when she discovers that I stay awake all night, shivering from the cold at the edge of the bed. She tells Izy that Yaakov deliberately tears the quilt and enjoys blaming me for it, so that he can persecute me. Izy is overcome with anger and takes off his leather belt. He undresses Yaakov completely and beats him mercilessly, arousing the fear that the child will be permanently crippled (Izy's outbursts of anger are quite frequent and extremely unpleasant. He completely loses control). We watch in shock and helplessness. Irene tries very hard to stop her husband and in the end succeeds with great difficulty. I am happy that Yaakov was punished, but deep in my heart I know that Yaakov's revenge for his father's blows will speedily come, although I don't know what form it will take. The feather parties are stopped, but I still can't sleep most nights.

I have frost sores on my feet, especially on my toes. The sores aren't bandaged and the children kick, scratch and pick at them, pretending that it's unintentional. They know that I don't dare tell their parents, or scream, and they enjoy being able to hurt me with impunity. They indeed hurt me very much and I suffer without reacting. This is just one of their acts of revenge. I suffer many tortuous nights as well. I no longer have the strength to suffer them silently, but I also don't have any possibility of escaping them.

Another thing that creates tension in our communal bed is Irene and Izy's sex life. Irene and Izy have sex when they think we are asleep, but it also happens that their desire overcomes them and they have sex even when most of us are awake. I have no knowledge of sex, which was a subject not discussed in our religious home. Until a late age, I was convinced that babies are born when the stork brings them, and not as a result of physical contact between a man and a woman. I was completely unaware of having sex for pleasure. In spite of the fact that my two brothers were delivered at home with the help of a midwife, I believed that the stork brought them to my mother while she was lying in bed. When I was still living in my own home, I would sit by the window for hours, watching the storks that nested on our neighbor's roof. I wanted very much to see, at least once, how a stork holds a baby in its beak and carries it to someone's house.

With that level of sexual knowledge, everything I witnessed in the Bacher household was strange and frightening. When Izy and Irene have sex, everyone in our bed becomes tense, each with his own reasons. I am also tense and curious to know what is happening between them in that bed. The sounds and the movement and the moans coming from there are very alarming. I think that perhaps Izy is angry with Irene and is hurting her secretly, or that one of them doesn't feel well and I don't know what is happening to them. Often Irene cries out in a strange way and that frightens me to death. I don't know what they are doing in bed and why. In spite of the fact that I was born on a farm, I never once saw animals mating, and certainly not people. The Bacher children, on the other hand, know very well what their parents are doing and participate in the fun, each in their own way. I, who serve as an object of abuse for them, have to also suffer their sexual impulses on my body. When the boys are aroused by their parents' actions, they enjoy touching me grossly in my most intimate places, and I don't have the strength to oppose them. Their actions hurt and disgust me, and I struggle with them quietly, with all my strength, but don't always succeed in stopping them.

Of all the ways the Bacher children used to hurt me, this is the worst torture of all. Today, such acts would be considered sexual harassment, but then things were different. I suffered in silence. This was part of the price I had to pay in exchange for my life being saved.

Meanwhile a new hardship comes from an unforeseen source. The children did not cause this hardship, all the same it was very difficult to deal with. Fortunately for me, it releases me from the communal bed for a long period of time, and that gives me a measure of relief.

Mysterious Abscesses

In the beginning of the winter of 1943 the left side of my neck hardens as though some stiff lining has been inserted. This prevents any movement in the left side of my body. I can't turn my head and half my stiff neck is also swollen, making it unsymmetrical, and making me look grotesque. I can't reach a doctor, because of the danger involved. We don't have any medication for the swelling and we also don't know which medication would help me. In the meantime, my treatment consists of wrapping my neck in a scarf to keep it warm. The scarf doesn't help and doesn't solve the problem. Over the course of three weeks the swelling spreads to three different parts of my neck; a gigantic lump on the left side of my neck, a medium lump in the middle of my neck, where the vocal cords are located, and a small lump near the nape of my neck. The large one continues to swell and reaches the size of a large potato. It becomes red and shiny and then softens slowly and looks like rotten fruit. Izy periodically examines the lump and consults with Irene, but he has no suggestions as to how to help me. He doesn't have an extensive medical education, but as a dentist he understands more than the common man about medical issues. His major expertise is in the field of sterilization, which will be a great help to me later on.

Time doesn't cure or reduce the lumps. They are very painful and they look terrible. After much deliberation, Izy decides to burst the large one in order to examine what there is inside. For this purpose he sterilized his shaving razor and turns it into a surgical knife. In a jar he prepares some cotton soaked in iodine and dental sterile pads. The talk that I hear about the need to open the lump frightens me. The children wait curiously to see what is inside the infamous lump. They envy me all the attention I've been receiving and they also want to see how much stamina the "frightened rabbit" has. I, on the other hand, feel the need to prove to them that I'm not a coward and I want to behave like a heroine when the lump is being cut open, but I don't know if I can manage that. The fatal day arrives. Izy decides to operate. I'm quaking with fear, but offer him my neck. What will be, will be. I pray in my heart that the cut won't hurt too much, making me scream or cry. I don't want to give the children a reason to mock my weakness. To my great relief, Izy executes the cut so quickly that I don't have the time to utter a sound. A stream of green smelly puss bursts forth from the lump on my neck and reaches the ceiling. Izy comments that it resembles the eruption of a volcano. I don't know exactly what he means, because I don't know what a volcano is and how it erupts, but I understand that it's something extraordinary. Izy and Irene work a long time, removing and gathering the puss. They clean the abscess and squeeze it again and again until clear blood appears. I'm on the verge of fainting from the pain, but I don't utter a sound. In spite of the great pain and the disgust I feel seeing the green puss spurting from my neck, I sit silently on my torture chair. For the first time since I've been in the Bacher home, I win the admiration of the children for my stamina. After the puss is taken out, they spread pig fat on the wound. I don't know why, perhaps it has healing powers. However, the pig fat spread on the wound causes an infection and within a few days it becomes an enormous stinking abscess, which doesn't want to be healed at all. Several weeks later the lump in the middle of my throat also softens.

Now it is urgent to treat that one as well. Since the lump is located just above my vocal cords, Izy is afraid to cut the place with a razor, for fear of disabling my speech. Now that he knows without a doubt that there is puss inside, he wants to remove it and doesn't know how. The lump already resembles rotten fruit, flaccid, with a soft, wrinkled texture. It hangs in the center of my neck, and I look as though I have a turkey's crop. The puss is evidently seeking a channel of escape, and finds it in one of the canals of the large abscess, which is still open. We discover this accidentally when Izy presses on the lump. The more puss squeezed out, the smaller the ugly crop becomes and finally only a reddish, wrinkled lump is left. To this day it looks like a lined, burnt cookie, but in the course of time I've become less aware of it. When the little lump on the nape of my neck softens, Izy wants to remove the puss, but decides not to cut the place, but to tear it open with his fingers. He is careful not to injure the essential artery that passes there and he succeeds.

The infected abscesses torment me for over a year; however they also release me from the need to sleep with the whole gang in the same bed. For many months I sleep on the bench near the stove, and although the bench is narrow and uncomfortable, it's a real treat for me because my nightly torments, which are more difficult for me to bear than the abscesses, have finally come to an end.

Yitzhak and Yitzhak Surprise Us All

One winter night at the beginning of the year 1944, when all of us are sleeping soundly, we hear knocking on the window and men's voices asking about Masza Zunszajn – as I was called at home. We are all greatly alarmed, we are certain that our neighbors have come again for a surprise search. However, contrary to the previous times, they have the name of one of us and it is not clear how. Has someone informed on us? Irene claims that she has never heard such a name and she won't admit any stranger into her house, that isn't an official delegate. The men try to reassure her. They say that they are Jews, and that they don't mean us any harm, that they're friends and not enemies, and that the reason for their visit is that they heard I had fled to Irene's home after my family was murdered. One of them was a close friend of my father's and he wants to see me. He feels a moral obligation to my father to find out what happened to me, since my father can't worry about me anymore. Irene asks me in

a whisper if I recognize these voices. Although the voice of one
of them is a little familiar to me, I am afraid this is a trap and I'm
not prepared to say anything.

One of them says that his name is Yitzhak Geresh. I remember
that someone of that name was a friend of my late father, but
even that doesn't reassure me. I don't want to be caught in some
kind of trap. Irene waits for me to answer and I am silent. I won't
be the one to decide if she should admit them into the house
or not, although they seem to be trustworthy. I don't know how
long the negotiations lasted. My experiences since my family
was slaughtered have made me skeptical about human behavior.
I am finally convinced that they're Jews when they say the
Jewish slogan, known to me from home, "Amcha" (Your People),
The slogan dissolves all my doubts. I tell Irene that they must
be Jews. I also halfheartedly admit that I recognize one of them.
When Irene opens the door, we witness a scene that we never
dared to dream of. Two Jews armed with rifles enter the house
as though there is no war, as though they have no fear of the
Germans or anyone else. We are stunned. I start to cry. Others
cry too, and even Izy, who usually restrains his emotions, has
tears in his eyes. We inundate them with questions. They come
from the big, outer world, and probably know a great deal about
what is happening on the various fronts. They also ask us many
questions, especially my father's friend. He asks me about my
family, about his sister's family, who were our neighbors and
dear friends and about all the Jews of Wereszczyn. Unfortunately,
I have no soothing answers; I know that not one of them was left
alive. We ask about their current lives, where they are hiding,

how they acquired weapons and how they dare carry them about openly. We also ask them if they know of other surviving Jews and how many there are.

Until this visit, we were certain that we were among the few remaining Jews alive in Poland after all the news we received about the terrible murders the Germans committed in our area. We learn from them that there are twenty Jews hidden in the attic of a Polish woman, in a village named Garbatowka in our area. Among them, are two whole families that survived, along with their little children. They also know about Jews living in the forest; those who are alone and those who are partisans fighting against the Germans, but they have no direct contact with them. They bought their weapons at a very high price, but the guns award them security and power. They buy food at gunpoint for Jews in hiding and pay the full price. They present themselves as partisans and threaten the farmers with the revenge of the other partisans if they are harmed or refused food.

Yitzhak Geresh, my father's friend, tells us that after the annihilation of the Jews in Cycow, where he had been living, his, daughter, a baby of six months, and his nine-year old son were the only survivors besides himself. His other son died in Sobibor after being caught in the outskirts of Wlodawa at the time of the last expulsion. He, himself, succeeded in escaping. After the death of his wife, he placed the little baby in the care of a farmer's wife, an acquaintance from a neighboring village, who was nursing her own newborn baby. The farmer's wife agreed to nurse his baby, as well, but for a high price. He pays for the upkeep of the baby in gold and sometimes, when necessary, with threats at gunpoint. Yitzhak Geresh's baby girl was nursed with her Polish twin for over three years, and grew up with him like a sister in every way. Actually, she was with the farmer's wife until the end of the war, despite the fact that her father was liberated almost a year before, in July 1944.

This unexpected meeting is a very joyful one. Izy opens bottles of alcoholic beverages in honor of the occasion and Irene serves refreshments. I sit on Geresh's lap, happy for the first time in a very long while. I feel exceptionally close to these two Jewish men, as though they are part of my family. I learn from this meeting that there are some Jews still living, among them, Jews carrying arms and defending their lives honorably, walking about freely at night and not sitting hidden like mice under the ground, as we are. Izy is proud of his revolver and tries to show them that we, too, are prepared for a struggle when needed. He announces proudly that if, God forbid, we are discovered and are in danger of harm, we will be able to choose how we want to die.

The two Yitzhaks inform us of the advance of the Russian army on the eastern front. They claim that most of what is written in the official German newspapers are lies. One must read the newspaper upside-down. When they report that the Germans are fighting heroically somewhere, it's a sign that they are on the brink of collapse. When they write about a tactical abandonment of a particular place, it means that the Germans are retreating. Our visitors claim that defeat of the Germans is imminent and instill in us great hope that our liberation is approaching. It is agreed at that same meeting that the oldest daughter of one of them, who is suffering terribly from problems with her teeth, will come to us one night for treatment. The meeting ends in the early hours of the morning when all those involved – Roza, Izy, Irene, and I, are in high spirits and with hope for a better future.

The other children continue to sleep despite the extraordinary occasion. They're world is completely different from mine. After the war, Yitzhak Geresh built himself a new life and was blessed with many happy years. Tragically, the other Yitzhak and his thirteen-year-old son were killed by nationalistic Poles in the forests of Wlodawa – when they were on their way to obtain food in the neighboring villages.

Clothes and Ghosts

During the period of mass murders by the *"Einsatzgruppen"* (German SS para-military death squads), the local inhabitants looted piles of clothing taken off the dead bodies and many of them became wealthy from the sale of these clothes. I see this with my own eyes when farmers begin to come to Irene to sell her these clothes. Irene, who earns more than enough money from her dentistry, than needed for her family's immediate needs, is investing large sums of money in these looted goods. She buys clothes, expensive bedding, towels, underwear and other items. Some of the purchased items are for immediate use, and some are saved for better days after the war. She sorts out the goods, and what is destined for future use is packed in bundles and kept in the bunker, with us. Irene buys clothing stolen from the dead of a recent massacre in Trawniki, clothes that are still bloody.

To my amazement, Irene buys these clothes without any hesitation. She washes them calmly, dries them, and prepares them for storage. I am shocked when I see the water colored by the blood of the murdered. I am helpless. I don't dare comment on this to Irene. I can't explain to her how demeaning and immoral that purchase is. As a sign of protest, or perhaps because of the smell of the blood, my body revolts and I begin to vomit. Irene doesn't understand what happened to me, what illness suddenly overcame me. To this day I cannot forget the smell of the blood. Until that day, I was capable of being in the bunker together with images of the dead people who had worn the clothes stored there, without being afraid of them, but from the day I saw the blood in the laundry water, I began to have terrible nightmares.

During the long hours of sitting in the bunker next to the bundles of clothes, I see masses of ghosts. It's as if the people who wore those clothes, come out of them and hover in the dim air of the bunker, each at the moment of his death. Ghosts of men, women, children and old people scream, cry, and plead for their lives or are struck dumb with fear. They surround me on all sides, as though they are delivering a message to me that I don't know how to interpret. I press against Roza's body in my fear without telling her what I'm experiencing and why I am now more afraid than I usually am. I feel that if I tell her what's happening to me, she will think that I'm out of my mind. I am angry with Irene, I don't understand why she doesn't relate to the clothes of the dead as Roza and I do. In her eyes, those clothes are simply goods she had the opportunity to buy. Roza and I never say anything to Irene about the matter, but the act of buying the belongings of people murdered is to us a blow and an insult to our Jewish soul. We expect her to show more sensitivity in relation to those clothes, as the wife of a Jew, whose blood runs in her children's veins.

One day, among the things being sold, is a red flannel dress with pretty flowers embroidered on it. Irene is very excited about the dress, especially since it is very large and she can make three dresses out of the material for her three daughters and for me. The idea of this new dress doesn't make me happy. On the contrary, it poses a great problem: I'm afraid to say that I won't wear a dress stolen from a dead Jewess. I'm absolutely incapable of wearing such a dress. The days the dresses were being sewn were a nightmare for me. In my heart I pray that something will happen and I won't be faced with the test of wearing a dress belonging to a dead Jewess. I hope in my heart that something will happen to the dress; that the material will disintegrate in the process of sewing, or be burnt to a crisp or, as far as I'm concerned, just taken by the devil, so long as my skin won't have to come in contact with it. There is no one I can tell about how that dress disturbs me. It seems to me that even Roza won't understand me this time. I've learned from experience that there are things adults see in a very different way from the way children do. Roza tells me many times that one must learn how to differentiate between important and trivial things, and not get upset about everything. But the things that are important to one of us are not always important to the other.

Every time I think about the dress, I see before me the disintegrating body of the owner with tears of blood streaming out of the orbits of her eyes. It's a frightening, repulsive and pitiable sight, and I promise her not to dishonor her memory by wearing a dress made from her clothing. I feel that she wouldn't want that. The first dress was sewn for Ada, the daughter who is one year older than I am. She is very happy with the dress. She thinks it is beautiful and claims that the flannel material is very pleasant on the skin and is as soft as velvet. The second dress was made for the eldest daughter – Karin, and she, too, enjoys the softness of the flannel and is very happy with the dress. Then it is my turn. Although the only dress I have is the one that was made for me in Zaluszce, with the materials we brought from the basement in Wereszczyn, I know that I must avoid wearing this new dress. I feel that I'm not capable of wearing it, that something bad will happen to me if it touches me. I have no logical explanation for what actually happens in the end. Perhaps nature or some supreme power comes to help me. Irene sews my dress as enthusiastically as she sewed the dresses for her daughters. I become more and more troubled as the sewing progresses. When Irene finishes sewing and ironing the dress, satisfied with her handiwork, she tells me to take off the old dress and she puts the new flannel dress on me. I don't look happy as her daughters did when they put on her creations; a great disappointment for Irene.

Shortly after I put the dress on, I feel itchy and burning sensations and I'm extremely uncomfortable. Within only a few minutes I break out into a strange rash; many red Itching blotches spread over my skin. I start to scratch until I draw blood and my whole body trembles. It's as though I'm delirious. Irene looks at me in amazement and doesn't understand what's happening. I tell her that something awful is happening to my body and I must take the dress off. When I take it off, revealing my awful looking body covered with rashes and red blotches, I don't have to find any excuses for not wearing the dress. Irene concludes that I'm allergic to the flannel material, and I'm saved. Irene is very sorry, but I'm happy to get back into my old dress made from our store of materials. For me it still has the scent of the home that was taken from me.

By the Light of Glowing Embers

The long winter nights are a time of grace for the three inhabitants of the dark bunker. Irene and the children go to bed early, after their daytime activities, and we are awake. That is when a special ambience is created in the bunker, experienced and shared just by the three of us. Everything is quiet, the embers in the stove glow with a golden light; Izy, Roza and I sit by the warm stove in a mysterious, dimly lit atmosphere and undergo a kind of metamorphosis. We eradicate our present lives, are temporarily released from the constant fear of strangers, and pass into another world – a Jewish world where everything is filled with wonder and beauty. Izy and Roza are changed in my eyes. They are more beautiful, nicer and more agreeable, and I then feel a greater love for them, stronger and more unique than ever before. Izy's eyes shine with a special light coming from within and he begins to tell us stories from his past. He tries to give us a message through his stories and tells us about his childhood and youth in his homeland, Germany. He especially wants us to know about the Jewish world he lived in there. At this time we still believed that we were among the few remaining Jews, and Izy, the eldest among us, feels a moral obligation, or a fatherly one, to teach us about the history of our People.

Izy, who was born in the city of Jena, comes from an assimilated Jewish family. He and his brothers studied in a mixed school, together with Germans, and in the course of time, they became fervent Communists in the Weimar Republic. Both of them received a Jewish and general education, and in addition they studied music and art. Although Izy is an amateur artist, an amateur violinist, and is very knowledgeable in the history of the period of Jewish integration into German culture, he is a devout disciple of Moshe Mendelssohn and the ideology of Jewish 'Emancipation'. Izy and his brothers had to escape to Poland with the rise of Hitler in 1933, because the Nazis persecuted them as "Communists". The story of the rise of Nazism in Germany (until they took over the government) is also the story of the changes that took place in Izy's family – until they departed from the city of their birth, Janeh, which he loved, and which still has a warm place in his heart.

Izy is well acquainted with the mysteries of the glass industry of his city and he tells us about "Jena Glass", which has special qualities, and also about the many devices used in medicine and in science that are made of that glass. He is proud of his city, despite the fact that it is an enemy German city. Izy teaches me about Heinrich Heine, the world-renowned Jewish poet. Despite the fact that Heine wrote in German, as a German, he didn't repudiate his Jewishness. Izy is a great admirer of Heine's poetry and regrets that he can't teach it to us. It's also from Izy that I learn about the Emancipation period and the Jewish world I knew nothing about from my home. We were part of the East European Hasidic Movement, which centered on the *Baal Shem Tov* and his deeds, and for me that's what Judaism was.

In Izy's stories I also hear about the German literary giants. He enthusiastically tells us how the Jews were integrated into all the facets of German life, to the point where they became more German than the Germans themselves. Izy especially idolizes Moshe Mendelssohn, the world-renowned Jewish philosopher. He tells us about his philosophical works in German, and about his belief that the Jews should take part in general world culture without losing their Jewish identity. He tells us about Mendelssohn's grandchildren, the great musicians, Felix and Fanny Mendelssohn. According to Izy, both were gifted composers, but since in those days women were not accepted as composers, Fanny's compositions were signed by her brother, Felix, with the addition of a secret mark, which could identify them as hers. Izy speaks a great deal about the great wisdom of Moshe Mendelssohn, of whom it was said, "From Moshe, until Moshe, there's never been one like Moshe". Izy speaks about his longings for Germany, the land of his birth, as he knew it before the rise of the Nazis. In these nighttime stories, we embark to worlds completely different from the one we live in now – to the world of knowledge, freedom, brotherly love, and Jewish pride. We temporarily escape into a dream world, which awards us a few hours of grace.

These were moments of extraordinary happiness for me, a tenant of the dark hole, who lives in constant fear of the same Germans, who, according to Izy's stories were the most enlightened people of all Europe. I didn't understand then, and still don't understand, how these enlightened Germans changed so drastically that they became professional murderers during the period of the Holocaust. When I grew up and learned a bit, I discovered that Izy's stories were true and not the fruit of his imagination. The heroes of Izy's stories frequently appeared in my textbooks, and I was grateful for the early acquaintance I had with them through Izy.

One of the stories about Moshe Mendelssohn became particularly engraved in my memory. Its romanticism enchanted and excited me greatly. It's the story about the philosopher's love for a beautiful girl, who eventually became his wife. Mendelssohn was not a good-looking man. There was nothing in his appearance to make an impression on a beautiful young girl, but his fate was to fall in love with a girl whose beauty was acclaimed far and wide. Mendelssohn courted her relentlessly. He tried to be in her company at all times. Sometimes, he tried to see her and not be seen by her, so as not to be a nuisance – but he followed her everywhere. Mendelssohn, who wanted the girl with all his soul, understood that the greatest obstacle in winning her love was his outward appearance. One day, as he sat by her in one of the most enchanting parks of the city, he summoned the courage to request her hand in marriage by telling her a special story:

"When I reached the Gates of Heaven and came before the angel who dispenses characteristics to the infant souls before they enter the world, I heard the bitter crying of a girl's soul. I felt sorry for her and asked the angel why she was crying so bitterly. The angel's answer was that God had given her a hunchback, short stature, and an ugly face, and the girl doesn't want to be born that way and therefore she is crying. I immediately told the angel that I am willing to exchange my attributes with hers and to receive all the defects that God had assigned to her, on one condition, that I would receive such a high level of intelligence that all my physical defects wouldn't matter compared to my mental abilities. The angel agreed to the exchange and here I am before you". The beautiful woman burst into tears on hearing this wonderful story, and immediately accepted Mendelssohn's offer of marriage. And I, who understood from the people around me that I was ugly, contorted, and looked like a scarecrow, learned from this story that if I learn and gain wisdom, my physical appearance won't hinder me in life.

The Mad Woman of the Village

After the visit of the two Yitzhaks, Roza and I crave to leave the Bacher family and to join the Jews hiding in Garbatowka. I don't know and Roza never told me, what her reasons were for leaving. Perhaps they were the same as mine, perhaps not. My reasons are very clear. I want desperately to get away from the Bacher family and the hostility of the children towards me. I am sick of sitting in the bunker like a mouse in its hole, when there is an opportunity to hide in a different way. I want very much to be with other Jews, to live as they live, to play with their children as equals. I want to be among people and children who won't taunt me, and I am sure I can fulfill that desire. For me, at the age of thirteen, it would be like exchanging hell for heaven. If I were to ask the Bacher family to let me leave, they would categorically refuse and I'm afraid to run away and endanger my life. According to the rumors we hear, the Russians will soon liberate us, and it would be a shame to lose my life just before the end. If our neighbors, the Poles were to capture me, they wouldn't hesitate to report me to the Germans, even if liberation was already palpable. Roza, on the other hand, thinks she can succeed in escaping and decides to do so at the nearest opportunity. In the beginning of spring in 1944, Roza has a plan of escape to Garbatowka, in order to join the Jews hiding there. She knows that if she asks the Bacher family for permission to leave, they won't agree for various reasons. But she tells me of her plans in order to prepare me for the idea of being compelled to live without her, since she knows that would be very difficult for me. She is also in need of someone to confide in, and I am the only creature on earth who can understand her at this time. She denies all my pleas to join her. She is not prepared under any condition to fulfill my wish and this hurts me very much. I can't understand or accept her reasons for this refusal, which are supposedly her concern for my life and my security. If the escape doesn't endanger her, why should it endanger me? But she argues that it is for my own good to remain where I am. It's very difficult for me to accept the fact that I am about to lose the only person I can take into my confidence about my distress and suffering. It's difficult for me to forgo the possibility of cuddling up in her lap when I'm distressed or frightened. I completely understand her desire to escape, but it hurts me that she is deserting me. With all that, I can't force myself on her.

As we wear ragged clothes, Roza needs to be equip herself with some better items of clothing, (which she does not have), so as not to arouse suspicion when escaping. She opens one of the packages of clothes and takes out what she needs, without Izy noticing. Her problem is acquiring proper shoes, since there are no shoes in the packages Irene buys for the tenants of the bunker. We don't wear shoes, so as not to make noise when we jump into the bunker. We wear thick woolen socks in the winter and lighter socks during the summer. We haven't worn shoes for the entire period of hiding, (that is for two years.) All Irene's children have shoes, albeit shoes with wooden soles, for those are the only kind available at the time in our area. Leather boots are very expensive and rare, and only Clara has a pair. She received them for her 13th birthday, as a Bat-Mitzvah gift, and everyone is envious of her. Any one who owns such a pair is considered to be of very high status, aristocracy. As her only possible course of action, Roza plans to steal the shoes of one of the children. She plans to leave very early in the morning on a particularly rainy day. Roza has a typical Jewish-looking face, dark shiny hair, large dark eyes and an eagle nose. Any Pole who sees her will immediately report her to the Germans because of her Jewish appearance.

I don't know what was going on in Roza's head in the early morning of the day of her escape. When she wakes me, she is already wearing the clothes she prepared and is ready to leave. She looks so different that I hardly knew her. She looks to me like half a lady and half a peasant. Her clothes are creased, though they do look urban. However, her head and face are those of a peasant – wrapped in a large kerchief that hides everything but her eyes. If I were to accidentally bump into her, even I wouldn't recognize her. And again, I don't know who is more afraid of this same morning: she, the escapee, or I who remains without her. Roza says goodbye without any sign of emotion and quietly leaves the house without anyone noticing. I don't know what to do. The door has to be closed from within after she leaves, so that no stranger can surprise us, but I am afraid to do that. If I shut the door, it will be clear to the Bacher family that I knew about Roza's plans and they will be very angry that I didn't reveal anything to them– in light of the fact that her escape endangers the entire family, if she is caught and the secret of our existence is revealed. On the other hand, leaving the door open is no less dangerous since some peasant suffering from a toothache might surprise us in the morning and discover Izy sleeping in Irene's bed, and me in the children's bed. The fear of the family's reaction to my cooperation with Roza paralyzes me. I lie shivering in bed and do nothing. I pray to God that someone in the family will wake up and discover the open door before some stranger enters the house. The possible reaction of the family frightens me so much that I would rather die than reveal my involvement in Roza's escape.

As fate would have it, just on that particular day, the crazy woman of the village has a toothache. She arrives at the house, bursts inside through the open door and wakes everyone with her screams of pain, "Why are you still sleeping?" she screams, "It's already late and my tooth hurts terribly, get up quickly and help me!" Everyone in the house wakes up in alarm; Izy gets under the blanket so that he won't be seen, Irene gets out of bed and apologizing all the while, she pushes the woman out. She asks her to wait until we all get dressed and until she organizes what is needed for the treatment of aching teeth. Izy and I jump into the bunker. Of course, no one finds Roza anywhere in the house, but in the current situation there is no time to look for her, and I am overcome by fear and guilt. The children dress very quickly that morning and arrange everything in the house within minutes so that Irene will be ready as quickly as possible to attend to the crazy woman's tooth, and also to subtly find out if the woman noticed that there was a man in bed with her. When the treatment of the unexpected guest's tooth is completed, the woman is sent away, and a major family investigation commences. The children are asked if they know where Roza is, and of course I'm asked as well. The children claim that they have no idea, but "the rabbit", meaning me, probably knows and is hiding the information. I emphatically deny that I have any information about Roza's whereabouts. I stubbornly claim that I know nothing about Roza's plans or course of action. One of my arguments is that Izy, who sits in the bunker with us, doesn't know where she is, so how can I know where she is? The family is suspicious of me and thinks that I am hiding something from them. They are aware of the close relations between Roza and me, and don't believe what I say; however they can't prove anything.

Because of the fear that the crazy woman saw things in the house that she wasn't meant to see, and that she will tell her family about it, it is decided that Irene will invite the men of that family to a feast, supposedly in honor of a visit home of Irene's partisan husband. Irene tells them that her husband is on leave from his partisan unit and that he brought many gifts and refreshments and that she is interested in having them meet him. Izy can't actually participate in the feast because he doesn't speak Polish well enough and also because he has no partisan stories to tell them. To overcome that problem, Irene organizes a sudden call for Izy to return to his unit to take part in a very important act of sabotage against the enemy. The next day when the feast takes place in our house in the company of the men in the crazy woman's family, Izy, the would-be partisan and I spend many hours sitting in the bunker. It is the first time that Roza isn't with us. I long for the warmth of her body, which was always near me in the constant dark of the hole. I long for her love and am very worried about her. In the meanwhile, upstairs, wine is being poured like water, slices of pork are being devoured and Irene is talking about her husband's acts of bravery. The purpose of these stories is to discourage the Poles from doing anything to harm Irene, because they are very fearful of the revenge of the Polish partisans.

Roza and Rivka

Life without Roza is very difficult for me. I must always have someone to love me. In the cold, dim bunker I have no one to cuddle up to, to keep warm, no one to console me, no one to calm me when the children are cruel. I am completely withdrawn from the outside world, to the point where the thunder of the canons heard in the distance; announcing the retreat of the Germans, don't succeed in bringing me any joy. My sadness grows from day to day. I feel an abysmal loneliness, although nothing has changed in my life besides the absence of Roza. On one night in the spring of 1944 there is knocking on our door, without any prior notice. In the doorway stand two young women dressed like the local peasants. Their faces are covered with kerchiefs, protecting them from cold and hiding them from the enemies of the Jews. As always, Irene cautiously inquires who these visitors are, and to her great surprise she learns that one of them is Roza and the second is Rivka, the daughter of one of the two Yitzhaks who visited us some time ago. Both are suffering from problems with their teeth and decided to come to Irene for treatment, despite the dangers in making the journey. The danger of being caught by the Germans in this remote place is almost non-existent since the Germans were defeated on the eastern front and liberation is near. The major danger to Jews during this period is the local Polish population.

Both of the armed Yitzhaks don't take any risks, especially now, before the end of the war. They follow the two girls, despite their protests, all the way to our house in order to protect them. When I see Roza my heart fills with joy. I missed her so much. I'm even happy that she has a toothache to bring her here. I begin to hope that she will remain here for a long time, perhaps even until the liberation and I will be able to warm my soul by being near her. I rub up against her like a cat. I keep close to her and swallow her with my eyes, but I have the feeling that something very basic has changed in her. The Bacher family begins to interrogate her about her leaving, about her present whereabouts and accuse her of a lack of responsibility. How could she leave the house without letting anyone know, without asking someone to shut the door? They accuse her of nearly causing us to be found and reported. During this bombardment of questions, she turns to me accusingly and shows no mercy. She knows what awaits me afterwards, but doesn't care. She tells them that I knew of all her plans, that I was awake when she left, and that I should have closed the door. If anyone is to be accused of irresponsibility, it is me and not her. I am shocked by her words. She makes me responsible for endangering the family. According to her version, I am responsible for everything that happened after she left. She turns me into an irresponsible liar, and I, instead of enjoying her return, can expect to be ostracized by everyone.

After such disgraceful behavior on my part, the children, will be justified in teasing, pestering mocking me, and calling me names. My joy in seeing Roza again turns into a painful disappointment, causing a great deal of unpleasantness. I feel betrayed and lost. I can't believe that the secret of Roza's escape, which I kept so faithfully, has turned me into a scapegoat. The girl that came with Roza, Rivka, is Yitzhak's daughter. Their whole family has survived. She is sixteen years old and very beautiful. She quickly endears herself to everyone, especially to me. She has the eyes of a deer, black and shiny, radiating light, a love of life and kindness. I secretly and joyfully immerse myself in those eyes. She has full, red lips, and a mouth full of white teeth. When she smiles, everyone around her smiles. I like to put my fingers into her curly hair, so different from my bald head that I want to cry. I feel she is the epitome of beauty, and I love everything beautiful that I see.

Rivka is given the attic to live in and I request permission to be with her all the time she is with us. Being in the attic is like being in a palace compared to the bunker. I can see many things through the cracks in the attic wall that I never see from the small window of the house. I see vast green fields, part of a pine forest, several straw roofs of houses and I even see stork nests on those roofs. I hungrily take in everything I see. Previously I thought that there was only a cherry-tree near the house and a path leading towards it and away from it. Suddenly everything changes. In addition to the new landscape, there is light, warmth, good air and also sweet Rivka. Rivka doesn't tease and doesn't criticize. She accepts me as I am and gives me lots of affection. She also tells me many stories. I know that this situation is only temporary and I treasure every minute of pleasure I get from being with her. With her I feel some joy in life and I try to store my strength for the hard times that will come after she leaves. Although to a great extent, Rivka makes up for the disappointment in Roza, I've learned the hard way that one mustn't become dependant on one person alone. I become suspicious and withdrawn, and I decide not to expect too much from anyone. My relationship with Roza is 'correct', but no more than that. She has changed and I slowly learn to adjust myself to the new situation. The two girls leave us after two weeks, when their teeth have been treated. My holiday is over and the only consolation I have is the sound of the canons becoming stronger and bringing liberation closer.

Blazing Skies on the Horizon

In the summer of 1944 it was clear to everyone, even in this isolated corner where we live, that the Russians are defeating the Germans. We don't know when the war will end for us or if we will survive until then, but we do know that the German defeat is certain and that makes us happy. The skies on the distant horizon are painted the color of fire and at night we clearly hear the thunder of the canons. From week to week the canons sound nearer and nearer. But for us who sit in the bunker, nothing has changed. We continue to hide, even though the German defeat is already clear. Although our liberation is approaching, we are not out of danger, especially from our Polish neighbors. The Bacher children tell us that in the dark one can see flashes of fire in the sky and that the entire horizon is lit up in red like an endless strip of fire. They say that it is an extraordinarily beautiful sight and my heart aches to see the blazing skies. I want to feel and to see the approaching liberation with my own eyes but, unfortunately, that isn't possible.

Although we live some twenty kilometers from the Wlodawa–Lublin road, and the road leading to our village is only a bumpy side road, we sometimes see columns of German soldiers passing, their clothes ragged, hungry and with lusterless eyes. They beg for food and drink, but no one pays any attention to them. All of a sudden, the all-powerful soldiers of the superior race, who exterminated millions of people, have become beggars. I am unable to grasp the changes in the world order. Will we, the Jews that succeeded in surviving, be stronger than the Germans and be able to take our revenge on them? Beloved Mama in Heaven, do you know that I have the pleasure of hearing Germans begging for bread? Instead of easing up a bit and allowing ourselves some freedom, Izy decides that we must be even more cautious than ever, in order to prevent any mishaps. We now spend all our time in the bunker, without going up into the house at all. We don't want to get caught just before the end. We sit for hours in the dark, waiting for the day when there is no longer any reason to hide. Since my great disappointment in Roza when she was visiting us, I've been seeking some sort of consolation. Since my imprisonment prevents me from having contact with people, I choose a cute grey rabbit from their burrow, located just above the bunker's air hole, and she becomes my soul mate. I tell her about all my troubles and all my joys, and she listens with great interest. I am sure she won't disappoint me and won't mock me the way the people I live with do. I look into her innocent eyes and am certain she understands everything. I love her with all my heart, perhaps with exaggeration, since she is now closer to me than any other creature and must put up with me with all my shortcomings. I feed her, cuddle and kiss her. Her pleasant fur keeps me warm. I don't leave her alone for a minute and bestow on her the wellsprings of love that used to be reserved for Roza. I am not sure she is too happy with my gushing affection and I've probably caused her some unintended pain, but what could she do about it, poor little thing? I even jump into the bunker with her. There, it is much more pleasant than in the house where there are so many mocking eyes watching me. Her little body warms my body and my soul from within and without, and in the dark I am free to act as I please.

The war front comes closer to us every day. The whistle of the canon bombs can be heard clearly and we are surrounded by chaos. There is no official body to direct the behavior of the civilian population in the existing situation. There are no shelters, no information on what is happening around us. We exist in a vacuum. There is actually no governing body. The Germans are fleeing, the Russians haven't arrived yet, and the Poles don't know what to do. They're afraid of the Russians and equally afraid of the Germans. There is a rumor circulating that the Russian tanks are pursuing the retreating Germans, and destroying everything in their path. It is also rumored that Russian tanks run over houses with the inhabitants still inside. The villagers are in panic and no one knows what to do or where to hide until the danger passes. We also begin to fear that we might be killed now when the war front reaches us. I don't know what a war front is like. I imagine it to be an enormous Angel of Death spitting death indiscriminately in every direction, through gigantic holes in its skull. I imagine that in every place the war front passes, it burns everything to the ground and what the fire of the front doesn't succeed in destroying, the Angel of Death annihilates with a huge, one bladed scythe. Every time the approaching war front is mentioned, I shiver with fear. I know that its approach signifies something good for me; the retreat of the German army and my freedom, but I pray that it won't come too close to us so that it won't hurt us.

In the middle of July 1944, many German soldiers pass through the village in great confusion. They look ragged and there is no semblance of the infamous "German order". There is a constant uproar of tanks coming from the main road between the city Wlodawa and the city Lublin. We hear shooting from machine guns and the whistling of canon balls. The battle isn't taking place in our village, but to be safe the entire family joins us in the bunker. The rumor about Russian tanks deliberately razing houses to the ground with the inhabitants inside continues to frighten all of us. I don't know who spread the rumor, or if there is any truth in it, but even though we are all Russian sympathizers, we believe the rumor and are frightened.

On the twenty second of July the tanks actually enter our village. We don't know if they're from the German or the Russian army. What will happen if a tank crushes our house? Will we be crushed inside the bunker? We are all afraid, but the bunker seems to be the safest possible place under these circumstances. Despite the fear, we all crowd in there and wait. Time passes slowly and the furor outside continues. From time to time Irene or one of the children try to go cautiously outside to see what's happening, but they return in alarm very quickly and they have nothing to say to reassure us. The most important, and the only reassuring thing is that despite the war being waged outside, we are still alive and our house is still standing and hasn't crushed us.

Something very sad happens to me personally on that day. In all the confusion of the front passing through our village, my little grey rabbit is killed. To this day I don't understand how it happened. I guarded her carefully but it happened anyway. Evidently during the crowdedness and the pressure of everyone hiding together under the ground, someone accidentally smothered her. I couldn't even bury her because of the heavy bombing outside. My precious little loved one is thrown aside like a rag in the field beside the house. Confused and frightened, I think that I didn't take good enough care of her and I am plagued by terrible guilt feelings. Perhaps it is an act of fate. Her comforting role in my life must come to an end. A new era is opening before us, where she evidently will no longer have a role in my life.

On the evening of the twenty-second of July the village becomes quiet. The thundering of the canons becomes fainter and fainter until it becomes completely silent. We feel that the war has moved away from us. Irene decides to go outside and if possible to make a thorough examination of what is happening; what the meaning of this silence is and who is in charge now. Outside, there is no one to be seen and no one to ask. Irene goes to the home of the Mukhtar of the village. He is the only one who can perhaps give her a credible answer. According to him, the Russians have been ruling the village since the afternoon. The villagers are hiding in their houses. They don't know what to expect from their new rulers. In spite of the fact that the Germans have been defeated, one must still be careful. It is rumored that small groups of German soldiers are hiding in the forest and in the wheat fields that surround the village. They rob and kill everyone that crosses their path. When Irene returns with the glad tidings it is already dark outside. We are all confused by the sudden change.

In order to see if something has really changed, I request to go outside and to my great surprise, I am allowed to do so. For the first time in two years I go out of the house to breathe fresh air. I fill my lungs with air, a lot of air, and breathe so deeply that I almost begin to choke from all the air that I take in. I still don't understand the change that is about to take place in my life. I want to save a reserve of air for afterwards, because perhaps I will have to hide again in the suffocating bunker. It's so pleasant in the fresh air. I had completely forgotten its smell. Only someone who was imprisoned as I was, over two years in an airless hole, and in a smelly house where it was forbidden to open the only window, can understand the pleasure and delirium of my first breath of fresh air. Something that has been severely forbidden for so long, is suddenly permissible? It seems completely natural to be outside and to breathe the air freely at any time, but I had been weaned from this natural thing. After two years, I am permitted to look at the moon and the stars, whose existence I had almost forgotten, and their beauty surprises me. I smell the intoxicating fragrance of a summer evening, I hear the orchestra of crickets and other night creatures and my heart swells with pleasure. All this was taken from me for so long through no fault of my own.

Meeting the Liberators

On the day after the liberation, on the twenty-third of July, I awake very early and want to go outside again. I can't get enough of the outside. I want to see if this freedom is real and not just a fantasy. I don't have the patience to wait for the whole family to wake up. I want to see the sunrise. I want to see the forest and the fields, the summer flowers opening at dawn. I want to just run, I very much want to be a little girl again. For two long years I could never walk a distance longer than between the walls of the house. And I had completely forgotten what it feels like to run. After all, I was a little girl who loved to run about and play outside all day long. I get dressed quickly and am ready to go out, but Irene stops me. Outside there is still danger from the local people and she asks me to wait until others in the house get up. I'm disappointed, but accept what she says.

When everyone gets up, Irene tells us that she plans to invite the Russian soldiers in the area to a welcoming party today and she expects us all to help her. She wants us to celebrate the victory over the Germans with the Russians and to express the family's gratitude and support of our Russian liberators. Irene also wants to show me to them, the little Jewish girl that she saved from the Germans. Saving her Jewish husband is an obvious duty, but to save a strange girl is something else. I am to dress in proper clothes and not appear before them in the rags I've been wearing up to now. We'll set a table fit for a king, considering the poverty of those days: we'll serve home made vodka called "Samogonka", home made Polish sausage, smoked ham and fresh home-baked black bread. Izy dresses festively and wears shoes for the first time in two years. I, too, am wearing a skirt and a blouse for the first time in a long while. Although I'm bald and bare-foot, and still have sores on my neck, I feel festive and curious about the meeting. I had seen Polish soldiers before, and German soldiers too, but I had never seen liberating soldiers. I imagined these liberators as Titans, and not just ordinary human beings. If they succeeded in overcoming the Germans, they are capable of anything. They are probably very special, big and strong, good and beautiful, perfect in every way. When they arrive, I'm very surprised. They look like any other ordinary people, like myself. They're not particularly big or strong, nor are they especially beautiful. It was a great wonder to me that they truly succeeded in defeating the Germans. Irene introduces all of us to them and we toast a drink to our liberation. It's quite easy for me to understand the Russian language because of its similarity to Polish, so that we are able to communicate quite well. I am presented as the only survivor of my family and my village, who was clutched from the claws of the murderous Germans and remained alive due to the protection I found in the Bacher household. Izy, her Jewish husband is presented to them as a veteran Communist who suffered not only because he is a Jew, but also due to his ideological beliefs.

The soldiers eat and drink heartily and listen to our stories. They take an interest in me, the orphan, and they have a tempting offer for me, seeing that the Bacher family has five children of its own. They tell us that there is a large group of orphans in their unit, orphans gathered from the different fronts and they are willing to have me join them and be a child soldier just as they are. The children live with them as an independent group. They study, take care of themselves, play and are happy. Although they are always with the unit at the front, they are always kept at a safe distance from danger. They wear soldier's uniforms, but live like ordinary children. The army keeps them away from dangerous areas when necessary. Despite the great attractiveness of their offer, I don't accept. True, I would gladly part ways from the Bacher family, but I don't want to continue living in warlike conditions when I have the opportunity of being rid of them. In addition, I think it would be difficult for me to live among so many boys, since most of the children are boys. I don't know if I could get along with them, and I don't want to create new hardships for myself.

I remain with the Bacher family and after the liberation, I fall into the deepest depression I've experienced, since I was left all alone. So long as I had to fight for my very life, for survival itself, I didn't have the time to think about my future. But now the war is over, and for me nothing has changed. I'm alone as I was before during the occupation. True, I am now free, but what am I to do with this freedom? To whom will I go? Who will raise me? Who will love me as I was loved at home? Who will tend to my needs? Will I attain at least some of those things my mother always dreamed of bestowing on me? Will I return to live a Jewish life as I did with my parents? The longing for my family and my home are awakened with extraordinary force and drive me to distraction. I have no one to talk to about what is bothering me, and that makes it even worse. Liberation from the Germans hasn't changed much for me. Instead of being happy, having fun outside and enjoying my freedom, I sit in a corner and cry. Besides being able to be outside in the fresh air and not underground, everything remains exactly as it was before – The same harassment from the children, the same feeling of being a second-class child in a strange family, my inability to change the situation, all contribute to my deep despair.

Actually, this is the first time I realize the immensity of my loss. For the first time I understand that I will never have a home as I once had. Although I survived in order to make it known that we existed, and I fulfilled Mama's request, and I lived to see the fall of the Germans, I don't feel any joy in my heart. I feel that without a loving home like the one I had, there isn't much point in my existence. I am shrouded in renewed grief. Actually, before the liberation, I didn't have time to mourn for my family. I was in a constant struggle to survive. Now that I'm free of the struggle for survival I want the impossible, I want my lost home. Life has lost its purpose for me. My longing for Mama, Papa and the family is now unbearable.

Despite the fact that the Germans have been defeated and the government is now in the hands of the Russians, it turns out that the struggle for survival hasn't actually ended. The Polish nationalists, who have always persecuted us, now want to complete what the Germans didn't complete and they kill every Jew they see. We must flee from Zalisocze as quickly as possible, because we are in danger. The truth is that I'm not sorry we have to leave this isolated place. I have no good memories of it. I only had a few weeks there as a free person and I have no attachments. Most of the two years I spent there I was hidden underground and the fear of the local anti-Semites was so great that I'm happy the Bacher family has decided to leave. I hope that my luck will change with the change of place and my state of mind will improve.

On one bright morning two wagons that Irene had rented, appear in front of the house. We are all recruited to help load the wagons with the family's belongings, which had already been packed, and we move to the city of Wlodawa only two weeks after being liberated by the Russian army.

Roza and Geresh

Wlodawa of 1944

In 1944, after the liberation, Wlodawa – a city that was almost completely Jewish before the war – is now a ghost town. Almost all the Jewish inhabitants, and the Jews of the surrounding area, were killed in the Sobibor extermination camp. The few survivors who fled to the forests, the survivors of the Sobibor revolt and those from villages of the area, are now gradually congregating in Wlodawa and turning the city into a temporary asylum. The partisans, arriving from the neighboring forest, are carrying weapons, which gives us a sense of security when we come to the city. The weapons are needed for self-defense from the nationalistic Poles who continue to kill the surviving Jews wherever they find them.

When we arrive in Wlodawa there are already few Jews there, but every day brings new survivors. In the course of time, quite a large Jewish community is assembled. This community organizes all aspects of life within it. Most of the survivors coming to the city live in the former homes of Jews; the few homes that survived the burning down of the ghetto. A Jewish militia is organized with the approval of the Red Army. This militia takes responsibility, not only for the security of the people, but for other needs as well. The survivors are always looking for relatives among the Jews gathered in the city. They also seek human ties with one another, as a substitute for their families that were annihilated. There is a sense of brotherhood among us, the brotherhood of survivors.

One day I witness a very grave incident between a Jewish militiaman and a nationalistic Polish citizen. It was wondrous in my eyes and a source of pride that a Jewish militiaman kills a Polish citizen in the light of day, within sight of everyone, in the crowded market place. I am convinced the Jew was right in what he did, even though he took a human life. Finally the Jews, too, are strong and use their strength when necessary. The Jewish militiaman wanted to search the Polish man on the suspicion that he was bearing arms. Under the circumstances the militiaman sees this search as necessary and when the Pole resists, he fires. This incident creates tension between the two populations living in Wlodawa, however it serves as a warning to the many anti-Semites in the city.

When the Bacher family arrives in Wlodawa, we live in a wing of the house of a Jew named Sheftel and his little son survived the war with in a partisan camp. Compared to the house in Zalisocze, this apartment is like a palace. We have several rooms and there is no need to sleep in a communal bed. There is room to open a dental clinic, and we have a well-equipped kitchen and dining corner. It's a refreshing change for all of us. For the first time in my life, I see an electric bulb. I can't understand this wonder.

How can it be that you press a button on the wall and a light comes on by itself in a bulb in the middle of the ceiling? Until then, I was only familiar with kerosene or carbide lamps that give light when you light them by hand. Suddenly such an innovation! For a long time I'm afraid of turning on the light by means of the switch, thinking that perhaps a little devil will come out of the wall and I will get a burn or a shock. A large number of Jews are living in this large house with its vast backyard. Among them are partisans from the forests, survivors of Sobibor, and Sheftel and his son.

I don't remember the names of the people who lived there, except for Hepy from Holland. I don't remember what the circumstances were that caused us to sleep together. She is a Jewish girl from Holland, who participated in the Sobibor uprising and survived in the forest. It seems to me that our need for closeness is the real reason for our sleeping together, and not the lack of room. This close human contact is a consolation for both of us and I see her as a kind of big sister who needs me as much as I need her. Sleeping together contributes a great deal to both of us in alleviating our loneliness, which increases as life becomes more normal. But Hepy leaves the city very quickly – I don't know where she went – perhaps to Holland, and once again, I remain alone with the Bacher family.

Sheftel's house is big, made of wood, has a fenced-in backyard, and wasn't harmed at all during the war. I don't know who initiated it, but a short while after we arrive, a large public kitchen is organized for the survivors in the backyard. A gigantic boiler is placed on a tripod, beneath which there is a pile of branches, which supply the energy for cooking. Every day Jewish survivors gather there spontaneously. They sit together and tell the stories of their lives, tell jokes, sing songs of longing in Yiddish and in Russian and peel potatoes, which are the major ingredient of the soup. The atmosphere is amiable and brings about many friendships, romances and even weddings. This togetherness provides many of us with the emotional support of which we are in need. Irene's contribution to the soup is melted pig fat that she collected in huge amounts during the two years she worked as the village dentist. In Zalisocze she would buy pork and melt the fat. She would preserve the fat by pouring it into glass bottles when it was hot, closing them hermetically and burying them in the ground to keep them at a low temperature. When the Russians arrive in Zalisocze, she has over one hundred bottles of excellently preserved pork fat. The fat, potatoes and good will are the ingredients of a hot plate of soup for all the Jews in need of food. For many, this plate of soup serves as a lifesaver in the first days after their liberation from wherever they were. Most of the Jews arriving in the city are penniless and don't have the money to buy basic food for survival.

The pleasure of being together among all the Jewish survivors is a great comfort to me. The few young children who survived are a source of joy to all. I, too, who have been left alone, am the object of a great deal of attention from all the age groups. The warmth of the other survivors is compensation for the hostility of the Bacher children. Once again I begin to believe in myself. The Jews who served in the Red Army come to us at every opportunity, and like all of us, try to find relatives among the survivors. The Shabbat gatherings in Wlodawa are particularly beautiful. On each Shabbat, we assemble in someone else's apartment, greet the Shabbat and sing soulful songs, mostly in Yiddish. I remember some of the songs I learned at those Shabbat celebrations to this day, and they are an addition to the repertoire my mother bestowed on me during her short life.

Eastern Poland has been liberated and the war is essentially over for us, but everything in our lives feels temporary. We are waiting for the war to fully end, in order to begin our new lives. In the meantime, each of us fights his own private struggle for survival. I feel that I must make a change in my life. In order to feel my own liberation, I must leave the Bacher family. I don't know if another place will be better or worse, but I know that my situation will be different and I am in need of a change. It's clear to me that they won't give me permission to leave them, so I decide to leave without their permission, in other words to run away.

Planning a Getaway

Shortly after our arrival in Wlodawa, Izy is conscripted into the Red Army. Despite the fact that he is almost forty years old, he is evidently essential to the army due to his being a dentist and to his fluency in German. Izy's absence leaves me completely at the mercy of the bullying children and I lose the one person I love in the family. When the fear of Izy's belt disappears, there's nothing to restrain the children and I feel I must free myself from them. The straw that breaks the camel's back is when Irene sends her children to school at the beginning of the school year, and leaves me at home to help her with all her tasks. From Irene's point of view and that of the children, it's reasonable that they go to school and I don't, because I already know how to read and write and they don't. But from my point of view this decision is a blatant injustice to me. Irene's discrimination against me hurts me deeply and angers me. I wasn't able to start school when I should have, because of the war, and now that the war has finally ended and I have the opportunity to realize my dream of learning, it's barred from me because of the selfish and unjust considerations of the family.

The idea of getting away from them becomes prominent in my thoughts. I don't know where to go or to whom. I wait for a suitable opportunity, and fate soon arranges such an opportunity. In one of the Shabbat gatherings, I hear that Roza has arrived in Wlodawa and is working for Yitzhak Geresh, who visited us during the Nazi occupation. It's clear to me that the only person I can go to without informing her beforehand is Roza. Despite the strained relations between us resulting from her visit during the occupation, I trust her not to turn me away, even if my arrival does not exactly please her.

After making the decision where to go, there is still another obstacle to overcome. My parents' documents, which I found on the grave and the family pictures, aren't in my possession. Irene is hiding them from me and I have no logical explanation why. Without those treasures, the only ones left to me from home, I can't move from here. I begin to secretly look for my treasure, but find nothing. Despite the fact that I am often home alone, especially in the morning, when the children are in school and Irene is working, and I am relatively free to do as I like, I still don't succeed in finding them. In order not to arouse any suspicions and in order to have access to all kinds of secret corners in the house, I announce the beginning of a clean-up campaign to clean all the places that we usually don't get to. I have a lot of time in the morning when the children are at school, and I don't want to sit around and get bored. I begin to clean all the cupboards, one at a time, and I wipe the shelves that are hard to reach in routine house cleaning. I empty and clean all the drawers in the house and examine every place that the documents and photographs might be hidden. My diligence surprises the members of the family but no one objects to what I am doing, and they even compliment me for it, since I find all kinds of things they've been looking for. My campaign lasts about two weeks, and when I am about to give up, I find what I've been looking for in a completely unexpected place. Under a pile of torn socks that no one wears anymore, in a drawer of a cupboard that almost no one ever uses, I find a hidden envelope and inside it is the treasure I so much wanted to find before my escape.

The moment my treasure is in my possession, I hug it to my chest and have the feeling that I'm again connected to my family. Now I can do whatever I like. I leave the Bacher household without any qualms and run with all my might in the direction of Roza's home. There happened to be no one at home when I left so that I didn't have to invent any explanations or excuses. I know where Roza lives, because several days beforehand I inquired among my acquaintances, so that I would know exactly how to get there when the time came. Wlodawa isn't an especially big city and the Jews, who gathered there, are concentrated in the same area, and everyone knows everyone else. Geresh is well to do financially, while most of the other Jews are paupers who have nothing. He is a well-known and respected figure, whose quick success is much talked about. Many envy him and gossip about how he behaves like a lord and employs a household manager. His lodging is located in a very central place in the city, near the market square, so that I needn't make a great effort to find him and Roza, his household manager

I arrive at Roza's house breathlessly, with my heart throbbing, and burst inside. I tell her that I ran away from the Bacher family and have come to live with her. I completely ignore the strained relations that existed between us the last time we met, and pretend that everything has remained as it used to be between us. Since she is the only person I know whom I can come to, I don't ask if it's possible or request her permission. I state a fact. It doesn't even occur to me that she might not be able to accommodate me. After all, the house doesn't belong to her, but to her employer, and he may object to my staying. It's true that he was a friend of my father's, but that fact doesn't oblige him to take me in. I don't request his permission. I simply place myself in Roza's hands and she, who knows how difficult it is for me with the Bacher family, accepts me without any protest.

Later on I learn that the situation isn't so simple and that my unannounced arrival, without the landlord's permission, causes Roza quite a bit of trouble. I had disregarded this possibility completely, because I had absolutely no choice. I must give her credit for trying to keep me from knowing about the problems I caused her.

A New Place

The war continues somewhere in Europe, far from us, and this doesn't occupy my thoughts at all. I don't know that people are still being killed at the front, or that the German killing machine continues to operate at full speed. Actually, at the time I was liberated, the Jews of Hungary were just beginning the hell of the extermination camps. I am so absorbed in myself and in my own problems, that I don't take an interest in anything else. Before the liberation, I would read the newspapers, listen to Izy's political analyses of the situation at the various fronts and wanted to be involved in every little change that was taking place around me. Now nothing interests me. I see my escape from the Bacher family as the beginning of my personal liberation and I want to take full advantage of it. Finally, after such a long time, I come to a home where no one plagues me, where I have a corner of my own. I sleep in my own bed, with no other children sharing it with me. I am no longer in a place where I feel like an unnecessary appendage, or like the punching bag of the household. This is such a dramatic change for me, that it's difficult for me to absorb it. Living with Roza is the realization of a dream that I had considered impossible. She treats me very well, provides me with food and clothing, with a bed in a hidden corner of her apartment, with a friend, and she even confides in me and tells me about her romantic secrets. I begin to connect with other Jews living in Wlodawa at the time. Only a few children my age survived, and if there are some in Wlodawa, I don't come across them. As a result I spend most of my time in the company of adult survivors. I listen to their conversations, and learn from them, but only very seldom do I say anything. I don't have the courage to take part in adult conversation, although I often have an opinion of my own about the subject being discussed. I have no opportunity to play with other children. Actually, I'm not familiar with the world of children my age. I don't know what interests a child living in a normal family, how he claims his place in the family, how he gets along with his brothers and sisters, with his parents, all the relationships I don't have. I think that if my family were alive I would feel I was in Paradise. Even today, now that I am a grandmother with a great deal of experience in life, I feel that an extended family is something perfect and holy, although I know that this isn't always so in reality.

A Hungarian friend of Roza's, named Imre, is courting her and has become part of the household and one of my best friends. He teaches me things that interest people his age, and it doesn't strike me as strange at all. On the contrary, I'm proud of it. He teaches me to dance ballroom dances, to sing love songs in different languages, including Hungarian, and he plays with me a good part of the day. Through me, he knows about Roza's whereabouts, gets closer to her, and receives compliments from her for how nicely he treats me.

Geresh, the landlord, who is also our breadwinner, isn't at home most of the time. He is occupied with his flour mill in Cycow and in the collection of money from those who use it. We are lords of the house most of the time, and we are free to sing and dance and have fun. He's not concerned with what we do there and I imagine he doesn't really know. Neither Roza nor I bother to tell him what we do in his absence. (By the way, Geresh's flour mill is active to this day. When I tried to go into it with the Israeli youth groups I accompany on their trips to Poland, I was harshly turned away. The new owners, evidently, were afraid we had come to claim ownership of the mill).

A Jewish man named Szczurek, owner of the building we are living in, and who survived with his little son, is also one of the visitors in Roza's house, and so far as I know he's courting her very intensively. I don't fully understand what these two men want of Roza, but I prefer the Hungarian suitor, Imre for her – he is young, tall and handsome, a good dancer and sings well. In my opinion, he has all the qualities to capture the heart of a young woman. His only problem is that he has no money. I imagine that this discourages Roza and prevents her from getting really close to him, despite my impression that she loves him very much. Of course my childish view of the matter doesn't take economic concerns into account. Love is holy in my eyes, above everything else. It makes me angry that Roza seems to favor the older and wealthier suitor, over our Hungarian prince.

Izy's Belt

When Izy comes home for his first leave from the army and doesn't find me at home, he is very offended and angry. I, whom he protected and nurtured, leave his household without his knowing about it, without his permission, and without any warning. After all, he never knew what I suffered in his house, how his children and his wife would make my life miserable, and he can't understand and accept my sudden leaving. When he learns from his family that I am with Roza, he decides I have to return home immediately. I don't know about Izy's leave from the army and also don't think much about what he will do and how he will react when he learns that I've left the house without permission.

One day Izy arrives unexpectedly at Roza's house, dressed in his army uniform. I think that he's come to show us how he looks as a Soviet soldier. When I see him, I want to hug and kiss him, to show him all the hidden love I feel for him and never dared to reveal in the presence of his family. But he is so angry that he doesn't even notice the love and happiness radiating from me. His face wears the hard expression that would accompany his uncontrollable bursts of anger. I recall those outbursts with repulsion. He would lose all reason and beat Irene and his children mercilessly. And now, judging by the look on his face, I fear that he is about to attack me, or Roza with the same fury. Despite the fact he hasn't seen us for a long time, he doesn't even greet us, but commands me to return to his home immediately, and adds that and if I won't do it willingly, he will force me to with his belt strap. His command takes me by surprise. I didn't expect it in my darkest dreams. I just recently began living a new life that I felt good in. Must I return to the hell I escaped from? I pray that Roza won't obey his command and I tremble with fear. It's very hard for me to disobey Izy and to disappoint him, but I am not prepared to accept his demand under any circumstances. He turns as red as a beet, shouts in fury and takes his belt off. I'm prepared to take the beating, but not to return home with him. I am unable to explain to him the reason for my refusal. I'm afraid to complain about his family and I don't want to hurt him. But I am also not prepared to suffer the humiliations that I suffered for almost three years.

At first Roza stands aside and doesn't interfere. She respects and loves Izy just as I do. We were all together through hard times for all of us and he was a kind of spiritual father to us – talented and intellectual, a mentor who taught us about life and an object of our admiration. Now, suddenly we become his opponents. But when Roza sees what direction the situation is taking and that I might be beaten, she decides to intervene.

First of all, she tells me to leave the house, and leave her alone with Izy. I hide in a corner of the stairwell, and anxiously wait for what's to come. Doubled up and trembling in my hiding place I feel as I felt during the difficult times during the war. Time seems to stand still. My fate is to be decided in there, and I have no idea what it will be. When I am no longer able to bear the pressure of my curiosity, I secretly steal into the house in order to hear what is happening. As I approach the door and press my ear to it, I don't hear any voices. There is absolute silence inside, as though no one is there. I cautiously open the door so that no one will see me peeking inside. To my great surprise, Izy is no longer there and Roza is going about her business as though nothing has happened. I understand that the danger is over, at least for the time being, and ask Roza what they decided between them. She never told me what was said in that conversation, but I understood from what she did tell me that the issue was settled positively. Izy was hurt and angry, but in the end accepted my departure. I can continue to live with Roza without fear, and I won't be troubled again by any of the members of Izy's family. My delight knows no limits. I fall upon Roza with hugs and kisses, endlessly grateful for her making it possible for me to stay with her.

Unfortunately, after that sad meeting with Izy, I never saw him again. Years later, we renewed our relationship through correspondence. Izy was very enthusiastic about my letters describing life in Israel. He wanted very much to come to Israel, but his family categorically refused to leave Poland. His letters were full of warmth and love. He kept me informed about all the family occasions and sent me photos with information about every new figure that appeared in the photos. His clan grew and I think that in spite of the guilt feelings he had about leaving Judaism, he had a happy life. Even when the diplomatic relations between Poland and Israel were broken off and it was dangerous to communicate with Israelis, he continued to write, using different codes to send and receive information. I'll never forget the congratulations he sent me after the Six Day War. It was essentially a code letter to find out if anything happened to me or to members of my family during the war. Unlike the other letters from the family, which were written in Polish, in Irene's handwriting – since Izy never was never fluent in Polish – this greeting was written in his handwriting in the Hebrew language and in Latin letters: "Le-Shana Tova Tikatevu". In the year 1987, during my first visit to Poland, I said my last farewell to him at his grave in Zielona – Gura.

A Surprising Marriage

After a while, Roza begins to accompany her employer, Geresh, on his business trips. I don't understand why, but don't have the courage to ask her. When they travel, I am left alone at home, at times for more than a week, and I run the household. I'm independent – I cook, clean and see to it that everything is in order. I'm proud that Roza and Geresh trust me and leave their belongings in my hands, without any hesitation. I often entertain Roza's suitors, who expect to learn from me where she is and why. I see nothing strange in leaving an eleven year old girl alone. I copy, almost to perfection, what Roza does when Geresh is absent. When Imre, her Hungarian suitor, comes in Roza's absence, I invite him to dinner and he dances with me, teaches me songs and asks many questions about Roza. Her older suitor, Szczurek also comes to visit me with his son and I prepare a hot meal for them, however, he comes less frequently.

To my surprise and great disappointment, Roza and Geresh return from one of their trips as a married couple. I had no clue that this was about to happen. I'm shocked by this development, but I don't dare ask her why she married a man twenty years her senior and not a young man her own age. It all strikes me as very strange and incomprehensible. I don't see anything in their relationship that could lead to marriage, at least not as far as I can understand. With the logic of an eleven-year-old girl, I understand that between two people about to be married there must be flaming love. I don't see that here, and suddenly they are man and wife.

Roza's suitors are as shocked as I am by Roza's marriage and cease to visit the house. I miss them a great deal. The house seems desolate without them. I particularly miss Imre, the young Hungarian, who was head over heals in love with Roza and, as far as I could tell, Roza was also in love with him. I loved Imre very much, but of course, in my own way: the adoration of an eleven-year- old girl for a, handsome young man who pays attention to her, and whom she sees as the realization of the ideal "Prince Charming". I was enthralled by his talent in dancing and singing, his ability to tell stories and to do all sorts of helpful things around the house. I am angry with Roza for not marrying him and I feel that she treated him shabbily, that she knowingly misled him. Many years later, when Roza visited Israel and Geresh was no longer alive, I received an explanation for the puzzle of her marriage to Geresh.

The household arrangements changed after the marriage. Geresh brings his daughter to live with us. She had been living with a Polish family from the age of six months to the age of three. I fall in love with her at first sight. I don't know what her real name is, but I know her as "Lalka", which means doll, and she really does look like a doll. To me she is the most beautiful doll in the world. I love her without any reservations. I play with her and take care of her, and she fills the vacuum in my life. She has lovely golden curls and black deer-like eyes that look at the world around her with curiosity and wisdom. She is very easy to deal with. She's not spoiled and doesn't cause problems in any way. It's pleasant to be with her, to listen to her sweet chatter and to answer her deluge of questions. The love between us deepens from day to day, and I am closer to her than anyone else. Our relationship is so good that the married couple has no qualms about leaving the little girl in my charge when they go on their business trips. Only when I became a mother in my own right did I understand the great responsibility they had placed on my shoulders when I was only eleven years old. At that time I didn't think there was anything wrong with it. Fortunately, Lalka accepts the absence of the adults and doesn't cause me any trouble. She grew up in a farmer's family without her real parents and she wasn't pampered. She practically didn't know her biological father and she saw Roza for the first time when she came to live with us. Thus she didn't particularly miss them when they were gone. She also doesn't show any signs of going through a crisis as a result of being separated from the family who cared for her practically since she was born. I have no explanation for her good behavior, but it was convenient for me. I feed, wash and dress her. She is like my doll that I can play with as long as I please. To a great extent I am a substitute mother and sister. Happily, nothing negative happens to either of us during our time alone together. It just serves to deepen our loving relationship.

Much to my sorrow, after I left the Geresh household, the family severed all contact between Lalka and myself. The reason why was never revealed to me.

In School for the First Time

Although the school year has already begun, I'm eager to go to school. So Roza decides to send me to school in the middle of the school year. I know how to read and write and do arithmetic from home because my parents had taught me. According to my age I should be in the fifth grade, but the school is only willing to put me in the third grade, with nine-year old children, and not children of my age. I'm very disappointed that the school appraises my knowledge at such a low level, but there was nothing I could do about it. Despite the fact that it's not exactly what I had hoped for, I'm very excited. For the first time in my life, I'll be going to school like any normal child; I won't let being in the third grade instead of the fifth, spoil that for me. I am apprehensive about meeting with Polish children, but my desire to learn is stronger than my fear. I'm overcome by curiosity. I'm already eleven and a half and I have never known what it's like to learn in an organized way; never experienced the atmosphere of a classroom. I can't wait to begin, and now, finally the big day has come. I'm sorry that my parents, who wanted so much to see me in school, aren't here to see me now. However, there is nothing I can do to change that.

Roza supplies me with a new coat, new shoes, a schoolbag with all the needed equipment so that I am ready for my first day in the classroom. All the other pupils are Polish nine-year olds. They are well dressed and nice-looking. Most of them come from well-to-do and caring families. Most of the girls have braids tied with well-ironed ribbons, as mine were at one time, and I envy them. I imagine their homes that weren't destroyed, as mine was. Most of them probably have parents, sisters, brothers, and grandparents – a full family circle – and I have no one. My whole world is different from theirs. I am the only Jew in the class. Although I am only two years older than they are, I have the life-experience of an old woman.

I judge everything from my Jewish perspective. I already know many of the things taught in class, and even excel in some subjects such as drawing, arithmetic and singing. On the other hand, I know nothing about Polish history, geography and literature. This doesn't worry me particularly. If I make an effort, I'll probably catch up. I have a problem, though in their religious studies. In the first two weeks of school, when I am given permission not to participate in those lessons, I go outside and play in the schoolyard. But my curiosity about how those lessons are conducted and wonder about the nature of their content drive me to try staying in class. In the third and fourth week of school, I request permission from the religion teacher to remain in her lesson. At first she refuses but, after much pleading on my side, she agrees.

The teacher of religion is in her thirties. She makes a lasting impression, and has a charismatic influence on the pupils. The first and only religion lesson I participate in, suffices for me for the rest of my life. The subject is the murder of Christ by the Jews. There is no historical background. The fact that Jesus was actually a radical Jew who fought against the way of life of his contemporaries isn't mentioned even once. On the other hand, the crucifixion by the Jews is described in minute and colorful detail, including the huge nails used to attach his hands and feet to the cross. The teacher describes the tortured look on the face of Jesus and the great pain the Jews caused him, so dramatically that all the pupils in the class, except for me, are in tears. The part the Romans played in the crucifixion is not mentioned at all, and the Jews are depicted as cruel murderers who showed no mercy to the Son of God. The eyes of all the pupils, filled with fury and hate, are turned toward me, the Jewess, as though I had personally murdered their God.

The religion lesson I participate in, which in my eyes is unmitigated anti-Semitism, astounds me. At the end of the lesson the children start hitting me and I hit back. In the eyes of these nine-year old children, I am the Devil's representative. All this takes place after the Holocaust when the blood of the victims hasn't yet dried. I learned a great deal from that lesson, though I may have exaggerated in the conclusions I came to. At my age everything still appeared to be black or white. This is the first time I understand the source of anti-Semitism. I understand that the Catholic Church feeds the Polish children anti-Semitism starting from early childhood. They absorb it from their mothers' milk. I decide that I don't want to learn or to be in such a place. A decision takes form in my heart, that I won't spend a second more than I need to on Polish soil, where the children are still incited against the Jews in every possible way. I return to Roza's house and inform her that I won't set foot in a Polish school from now on. Greatly agitated, I tell her about the lesson and what I learned from it. Roza's protests against my hasty decision are to no avail.

Despite my eagerness to learn, I terminate my formal education in less than a month. This was the first and the last time in my life that I went to a regular school. I decide that if the Jews will ever have a corner of their own in the world, that place will be my home. I don't know anything about Zionism or about any of the pioneer movements. The Geresh family never mentions the Land of Israel, or a longing for Zion. I come to the idea of Zionism as a result of my own life experience.

Painful Dreams

Life in the Geresh household is completely secular. The kitchen isn't kosher, Shabbat is not observed as it should be, holidays aren't celebrated according to Jewish law as they were in my home. Although Geresh conscientiously prays every morning with a praying shawl and phylacteries, it is very different from the way my father conducted himself. In our home all the Jewish laws were meticulously observed, and now that the war is over and life has become more or less normal, I expect the Jewish home I live in to be conducted in the same way. It upsets me that Jewish customs are not properly observed in the Geresh family. According to my childish logic it is inconceivable that someone who eats non-kosher food and doesn't observe the Shabbat devotedly prays to the God whose commandments he doesn't obey. In my eyes it is an attempt to deceive God. I, who grew up in a very religious home, believed that all Jews lived the way my parents did, and I can neither understand nor condone Geresh's duplicity towards Jewish law. I can do nothing about it, but this constantly occupies my conscience and my thoughts.

During this period I begin to have dreams about my father. I don't know if they're connected to my preoccupation with the observance of Jewish law or not. Every few nights, my father appears in my dream and preaches to me. I see how he pulls himself out of the dust covering his communal grave, as though all his strength is needed for this escape. My young father suddenly looks old, exhausted and weak, covered with blood and filth. He surveys me a critically, sighs, and suddenly undergoes a horrible transformation: the suffering, weary man turns into a lion growling at me in rage and distress. Although he has the body of a lion, he speaks like a human being and vigorously reprimands me for not carrying out the Jewish Commandments, the way our forefathers did, and the way that he and my mother taught me to do. I am tense and frightened by these demands that are repeated night after night, and I don't know what to do. I try to explain to my father in my dream that I have no choice that I'm obligated to behave in accordance with what's acceptable to the adults, but he doesn't want to hear this, and is not prepared to understand. He demands that I obey him, and I wake up from these dreams soaked in sweat, feeling afraid and guilty. I'm not able to change my way of life even if I wanted to, because I have no other place I can live. Everyday I beg my dead parents for forgiveness and say all the prayers I remember from home, but I feel that this doesn't satisfy them and that they don't forgive me. The dream comes repeatedly for a year, and pursues me even after I leave the Geresh family. I can't tell anyone about my dream, not even Roza. The message from my father hurts and depresses me, and I don't know how to cope with it. I can't change Roza's outlook on life, or her husband's behavior. They are my life support and I can't criticize them or make comments about their lack of religious observance. I'm trapped.

Had I known of any place where I could observe a Jewish way of life, such as my father demanded of me in my dreams, I would most certainly have gone there. I deeply desire to please my parents and to honor their heritage, but it was out of my control. It's ironic that afterwards, circumstances brought me into contact with other children who were educated in the spirit of *Ha'Shomer Ha'Tzair*, and there I gradually became completely secular.

Has the War Ended?

On the eighth of May 1945, a sunny day, although a bit chilly, the thunder of cannons is suddenly heard in Wlodawa. They sound very similar to those we heard during the war when the front passed through our village. I instinctively jump under my bed – the only available hiding place at that moment. I don't know if it's a pogrom, an attack by nationalistic Poles, or some other evil act aimed against us. Since the age of six I've known that the sound of cannon fire is a sign of something bad, usually war. It doesn't even occur to me that they might signify something else. Roza isn't home. I'm very worried about her and don't know what to do. I don't want to run away from the house alone, and also don't know where to run. There is no one near who can tell me what to do, so I remain in my improvised hideout and wait. When Roza comes home and finds me hiding under the bed, she bursts into laughter. She didn't realize how uninformed I was about the dire situation of Germany, which was on the verge of collapse. "Silly child", Roza says, "Don't you know that the Germans were defeated? Are you deaf and blind to all that's happening around you? What are you afraid of? Don't you understand that the war is over, that the roar of the cannons is a roar of joy and not of battle?!" I really didn't understand much then, because as far as I was concerned, the war ended when I was liberated by the Russians in July of 1944. I wasn't at all aware of the fact that the war continued for a year after that. We have no radio and no newspapers, Roza and Geresh don't discuss world events, so that I have no way of knowing what's happening. In addition, I don't take any special interest in what's happening around me. Actually, nothing interests me other than my own problems, needs and inner conflicts.

I don't understand the reason for celebrating the end of the war. This war caused so much pain, grief, and loss for so many people that I can't rejoice. Nothing was normal during the war. It is impossible to imagine the number of deaths there were. Death became the norm. Human kindness and compassion disappeared. I think that if the war has ended, instead of rejoicing, we should grieve for the dead and for those who remained alive, but broken, whose world lay in ruins all around them. The end of the war changes nothing in my life. I remain alone. I didn't even find one surviving member of my family, and I have no special reason to rejoice. But the adults are really celebrating. They're drinking alcoholic beverages and dancing in the streets. Just as I didn't understand their behavior in so many other situations, I don't understand their celebrating now.

Several months after the conclusion of the war, when the Russian regime became more stabilized, a rumor spread, saying the money which had been in use during the German occupation, would be changed. Everyone would have the right to exchange the old money for the new. I wasn't aware of the great wealth that the Geresh family had accumulated. One day many cartons and boxes are brought to the house. Only later did I discover that the boxes were full of paper money. I'm shocked. I had never seen, even in my most fantastic dreams, such a huge amount of money. I couldn't imagine that such a sum of money could belong to one person. The money is taken out of the boxes and arranged in rows on the beds and the tables. Roza and her husband, Geresh, with the help of some other Jews, untie the bundles of money and pack it in smaller packages, suitable for exchange. Later on I was told that Geresh offered other Jews in Wlodawa payment for exchanging his money for him. These Jews barely had enough money to live on and welcomed the additional income. I don't know what sums were involved, but it must have been a huge amount. Afterwards, when I had already left them, I heard that the Geresh family was wanted by the Communist Police, and had escaped from Poland in a private plane of their own.

Most of the survivors, who had gathered in Wlodawa, begin to disperse at the end of the war. Many of them move to the big cities of Poland, especially to those where new Jewish communities are being organized. Some of the survivors turn to relatives abroad for refuge, and an even greater number of survivors organize into *"Kibbutzei Hachshara"* (preparatory kibbutzim), through the *Halutz* (pioneer)–Zionist movements with the purpose of eventually migrating to the Land of Israel. The Geresh family decides to make a change and move to the big city, Lodz, where there is a large concentration of Jews.

Lodz

Details of my passage from Wlodawa to Lodz have been erased from my memory. That was literally a period of massive wandering: people traveling back and forth without any specific destination. They wander in every direction, seeking a foothold somewhere in the world – a home, a family, something to give meaning to their lives; the meaning that disappeared with the war. Trains are the main means of transportation. I don't remember seeing private cars, buses or taxis during that period. The only vehicles to be seen on the roads were military vehicles. Trains were the means of civil transportation and they were neither regular nor frequent. Masses of people crowd onto every train that appears, and the trains are overloaded. People ride on the roofs, stand on the passageways between cars, lie on piles of luggage and on the steps. The important thing is to travel from one place to another. We, too, push our way into one of these trains and travel with these masses of people in the direction of Lodz. I don't remember how long the trip took, or whether we changed trains or not. I only remember that we arrived in Lodz.

In Lodz, the Geresh family rents a two-storey house on a very busy street, Piotrkowska Street. I find the city frightening and confusing. So much of it is new to a country girl like myself. I see an electric streetcar for the first time in my life. It's a nightmare for me to cross the road because of the heavy traffic. I also find the crowds of people in the streets rushing in every direction both unfamiliar and frightening. To me, one who grew up in a small village, and the only city I had seen before was Wlodawa, feel that Lodz is a giant labyrinth and it takes me a long time to adjust to life in a big city.

With the move, there are no great changes in the life of the Geresh family. They follow essentially the same way of life in Lodz as they did in Wlodawa. I continue to take care of Lalka, Geresh's daughter. We spend most of the day at home, since we have nowhere else to be. We don't have any toys at home or a playground in the vicinity. I, therefore use my wild imagination to invent scores of games and stories for Lalka. As a matter of fact, Lalka becomes the center of my life. I am afraid to venture into the streets of the city without the accompaniment of adults, and the Geresh family has no time to go on outings. They are busy earning money and continue their travels to collect payment for the use of their flour mill. They are gone for longer periods of time because of the great distance between Lodz and Cycow. As usual, I am left alone with the little girl, sometimes for an entire week, with no means of communication with Roza and Geresh. They rely on me completely and it still does occur to me that there is something wrong with this. I continue to be a sort of little mother to her, with my accumulated experience in taking care of little children. I'm now more grown-up. I'm twelve years old. I take care of Lalka willingly and lovingly, and I don't consider the adults irresponsible for leaving me alone with the little girl. I see it as the normal behavior of most people and don't see it as unfit.

My Mother in My Dreams

When Roza and her husband go on their business trips they never inform me beforehand when they expect to return. But surprisingly, just before they return, my mother always appears in my dreams and leaves me various messages, which indicate that the couple is returning the following day. The first time my mother appears in my dream she suggests that I bake a cake and clean the house, because I will be getting visitors the following day. The suggestion seems strange to me, since I don't believe that it will really be so, but I follow her instructions, nevertheless, because I'm so happy to see Mother in my dreams. The following day, without previous notice, the Geresh family returns home. I think it's just a coincidence and don't see anything special about it. I don't tell Roza about my mother's appearance in my dream. It's very personal and I don't want to share it with anyone. Roza and Geresh are pleased to find a clean house and a fresh cake when they come home. They praise me for my diligence, but don't take it too seriously. They take my efforts for granted. On their next trip, several weeks later, my mother appears to me in a dream again and suggests to me to prepare the house as I see fit, because I will receive visitors the following day. This time I take the message very seriously and I prepare the house. I wash Lalka's holiday clothes and dress her in them, cook special food and wait with great curiosity to see if my mother's prediction will materialize. This time Roza and Geresh are amazed by all my preparations, without my knowing when they were coming home. They thank me profusely, but don't question me about how I knew they were coming home.

When the phenomenon repeats itself Roza asks me how I knew the day of their arrival. She jokingly suggests that I have spies watching them, for otherwise I wouldn't bake, cook and clean the house just at the right time. I unwillingly reveal my secret and tell her about my mother appearing in my dreams on the day before their return and about the messages she leaves me.

Despite the fact that Roza is a very realistic woman, she is very moved by the story and the two of us cry together, cuddled in each other's arms. I have no explanation for this strange phenomenon and I never asked a psychologist or an interpreter of dreams for an explanation. To my sorrow, since I been parted from Roza, my mother has disappeared from my dreams almost completely. She appeared again in my dream on the day before Roza's few visits in Israel.

I think about my mother a great deal until this very day. I still miss her despite the many years that have passed since she was killed. Almost every day, I consult with her, make requests of her and try to understand what she would think when I'm confronted with important decisions. Most of all, I try to be like her and to be worthy of her. She shares all my joys and my sorrows, but without Roza's presence I don't succeed in seeing her in my dreams, although I would really want that to happen.

A Second Rate Child

My life is now seemingly in order and I have everything I need. I'm living with a good, well-to-do family. Roza, whom I love, is near me, and there are no other children my age that can tease or compete with me for my place in the family. I dearly love the one other child in the house, sweet little Lalka, and am willing to do anything for her. She makes me happy and doesn't compete with me in any way. On the other hand, I'm not able to find any relatives, because most of them are no longer alive, and also because I know too little about my family and its history to know whom to look for and where. There is no place for me to go from here, even if I wanted to.

I'm completely detached from Jewish life in Lodz. I have no inkling of the great things happening here. I haven't met any other Jews in Lodz in all the time I've been here. I don't venture outside alone because of my fear of the big city, and the Geresh family doesn't socialize at all during this period.

After living in Wlodawa, where there was a lively Jewish community and Jewish guests in our home, I feel a terrible loneliness in Lodz. I don't meet any children my age. Despite the fact that during this period there was a large concentration of Jewish children in Lodz, I don't know of their existence or where they are. I assume that the Geresh family, occupied as they are with their own issues, doesn't think about the fact that I need a social life that I need things other than food, a bed to sleep in and Lalka's company. I spend most of my time with her, or with a book of Anderson's fables that Roza bought for me in the market place. While reading the book, I'm able to let my imagination take flight and become whoever I want to be, or go to whatever place I choose. I can change into anything or anyone, and be in countless places, and all this with great pleasure. Actually I live more in my imagination than I do in reality.

In mid-summer, 1945 I come down with a bad case dysentery. I've never had that disease before and don't know what it is. I have severe stomach aches and a lot of blood in my stool. I also have a high fever and I feel sick and very weak. Roza and her husband are not free to take care of me. They continue their regular routine, but they just make sure that Lalka doesn't get too close to so as not to catch the illness. I don't get any treatment and no doctor examines me. I am very annoyed by this. I feel neglected, abandoned and very sad. I have different expectations from Roza when I'm sick, and I'm angry with her for not giving me more attention. She and her husband leave me alone at home for days while I'm losing blood and I'm told not to eat anything but tasteless porridge they prepared for me. They promise me that within a few days, my condition will improve. I'm certain that I'm going to die from this disease, after having survived the German occupation. My self-pity has no bounds. I'm afraid that I won't succeed in fulfilling my pledge to commemorate my family, the reason I survived. I am so disappointed with the family during my illness that I again feel I'm a second-rate child, the way I felt with the Bacher family. I don't complain and don't say anything to the family, but I decide in my heart that I must leave at the first opportunity. I don't care under what conditions I will have to live, so long as I feel I am an equal among equals, and not like a second-rate child who depends on the charity of others.

And indeed, the possibility of finding another refuge quickly presents itself. Several weeks after my illness, some unexpected visitors come to the house. They are of Roza's acquaintances from before the war: an older man and his thirteen-year-old son. They are from Poznan, where Roza was born. They were knew Roza's family before the war, and were even among their close friends. Roza is very excited about this visit and has a long, nostalgic conversation with the man, whose name I don't remember. In the meantime I get acquainted with the son, Heniek. Meeting someone my own age is very exciting for me. My curiosity knows no bounds. I haven't met anyone my age since we arrived in Lodz and I want to seize this opportunity to find out everything about his life. After all, I don't know if I will have another opportunity like this. I bombard him with questions. I am not at all inhibited by the fact he is a boy. I speak about everything that comes into my head at the same moment. I feel that the dams I was unaware of inside me, burst open and I have no control of the flow. I want to know everything about him; where he lives, what he does, if he has friends and what do they do together, how does he get along with his father, what his inner life is like and if he feels the same loneliness that I do.

From my conversation with Heniek I learn that even when you have your parents, all your problems are not always solved. I always think that if my parents or someone from my family were alive, I wouldn't separate from them for a minute, and now I see that despite the fact that Heniek has a father, he doesn't live with him! His father sent him to an orphanage in Helenuwek, which is located in the vicinity of Lodz. Heniek tells me that his father wasn't able to take care of him alone and at the same time to support them both financially. Heniek isn't prepared to say any more about his life with his father and their relationship, but he is very happy in the orphanage. There he has many good friends who enrich his life. I am enthused by Heniek's story and I decide that if so many children find a home in the orphanage, even those who have parents, then I, too, will find my place there. I tell Heniek that I want very much to leave the Geresh family, but

I don't know how. Perhaps he can help me to be accepted in the orphanage? Heniek is excited by the possibility that I'll come to the orphanage and promises to help me with anything I need. I feel that I can rely on him and his promise sounds genuine. He also says that he doesn't think I'll have any problem being accepted. We liked each other from the moment we met. He feels older and more experienced in life and decides to take me under his wing and I'm glad to have it that way. After I consulted with Heniek concerning my future and I came to the orphanage, he indeed saw himself as responsible for me and helped me a great deal.

Shortly after Heniek's visit I have a long conversation with Roza and explain to her that I need friends my own age and don't see much chance of finding them while living with her. I also tell her about my need to change something in my life. I tell her about my talk with Heniek and his enthusiasm for the orphanage in Helenuwek, where he now lives. I don't make any demands or complaints. I just request that she willingly takes me to the orphanage. To my great surprise, she offers no opposition. I'm even a bit disappointed by this, although I truly want to leave her house. I evidently had believed that the attachment between us and my presence in her home were much more significant to her than they actually were. I collect my few belongings, receive money for the train ticket and after a rather cool parting, leave the house. I travel alone to Helenuwek, which isn't far from Lodz according to Heniek's instructions.

Helenuwek

Among Children like Myself

The orphanage in Helenuwek served as a home for homeless children before the Second World War. Before the war it was run by Romkowski, the infamous head of the Judenrat of the Lodz Ghetto. After the war the Jewish organizations intended to turn it into an asylum for refugees, but when they realized there would not be enough room for that, they decided it would continue to be an orphanage for the surviving children. When I arrive, there are already a great number of children, of all ages living there. They are divided into three age groups, with an educator for each group. There are sixteen-year-olds and some over sixteen, and also little children of four, who were born in the orphanage. A more or less suitable framework has to be found for each child. New children are constantly arriving. Compared to the way these children look, I look like a well cared for child from a good home.

The children arriving at the orphanage are survivors of different places and behave accordingly. Those from concentration camps have shaven heads, are very thin, and are plagued by nightmares. They hide every crumb of food they find in the folds of their clothes. They're constantly preparing for future hunger. The children from the partisan groups in the forests strut proudly about in their Russian Army uniforms, which they refuse to take off. They see themselves as fighters and sometimes fight against us as well. They have very close ties with the Russian soldiers camped in the area and feel very much at home there. The children who came from monasteries look healthy and happy compared to all the others. Many of them are still wearing crosses and secretly observe the Christian customs that saved them from the Germans. There are also children who have hidden with farmers, or like myself, hidden above or under ground, and they also have their own special qualities. Each child has his own behavior patterns, in keeping with his personality and his harsh life experience.

When I arrive at Helenuwek I am directed to the office to be accepted according to the rules of the orphanage. I'm certain there won't be any problem with my request for acceptance, but I am wrong. The head of the office doesn't want to accept me because he thinks that I've been living in a good place, with a family that has the means to provide me with good conditions. He asks me questions about where I'm from, my past and the place I lived before coming to Helenuwek. His conclusions are clear: I am to return to the Geresh family. There are many children on the waiting list, and they are much more in need of an orphanage than I am, because they're living in harsh conditions, and are alone and neglected. I have to make a great effort to convince him, and I even get Heniek to help me. In the end he agrees to let me stay in the orphanage.

When I am accepted and the formal registration is completed, I'm faced with another acceptance process, which is no easier than the previous one. The process of integration is strange to me, but I'm obliged to accept it. A girl from the older group is already waiting for me at the door of the office. She explains to me that the custom is for every newcomer who brings with him nice clothes or valuables, to put these into *"Shituf"* - the communal ownership of all the children. I don't know what *Shituf* is and I don't understand why I should give away the dresses Roza bought me. I don't like the idea at all, but I understand that it's a sacred rule and I don't dare oppose it. The one in charge of the *Shituf* is a girl from the older group who belongs to the Communist Party. She carries out the principles of equality and sharing within the framework of the orphanage. I still have photographs of my friends in the orphanage, dressed in the expensive clothes that Roza had bought for me.

In the orphanage I feel, for the first time since I've been alone in the world; that I am like everyone else, like all the other children around me. Most of the children are of the same class; orphans without a home, and we don't have to depend on personal favors for support. We are recognized by the authorities. Finally, I, too, feel that I am not living at anyone else's expense; that I am among equals. Life in Helenuwek is new and interesting. I make many friends; something I very much needed. There is a great deal of social and educational activity in Helenuwek. We put out a newspaper that reflects our active social life. This newspaper takes up a complete wall and many of the children contribute to and read it. It has different columns and gives every child the opportunity to express himself. I remember that, despite my young age, I also wrote for the newspaper. The newspaper doesn't concern itself with our difficult past, but rather with current events. There is some gossip; stories about couples trying to keep their relationship secret. There is a column that criticizes the management for fulfilling its own needs, and not ours. There is criticism of the kitchen that doesn't supply us with enough food. The criticism is usually disguised, because we are afraid of being punished, but on the whole, everyone understands what was meant. I particularly remember the humorous column, which I loved to read and I enjoyed the jokes in which we laughed at ourselves.

At Helenuwek I participate in ballet lessons for the first time in my life and I enjoy them very much. We do a lot of gymnastics, learn folk dancing, learn to sing songs in Yiddish and Polish and even sing Hebrew songs secretly. We listen to lectures on various subjects and participate in secret Zionist activities. We are so busy that most of us don't have the time to ponder our past. However, there are children whose emotional state is so fragile that they aren't capable of participating in these lively activities. I don't know if these children received any treatment, since the emotional damage caused by the war was not recognized anywhere; not in the Diaspora and not in Israel.

My greatest difficulty is the shortage of food. With the Geresh family I had enough to eat, and I almost forgot the periods of hunger during the war. Here, I am again hungry all the time. We are growing, active children. We have hearty appetites, but the amount of food allotted to us is small and rationed. There is even a shortage of bread. When we go to the kitchen to ask for a slice of bread we are driven away in anger. My stomach growls all the time. Beside the orphanage there is a fenced-in vegetable garden and fruit orchard. We develop expertise in breaking into them. Even I, the great coward am among the thieves. We devour every vegetable and fruit we find. Most of the yield of these gardens finds its way to our stomachs long before it ripens. In spite of this we don't suffer from upset stomachs.

When I start making friends with other children I have to tell them where I'm from, how I was rescued, and who my parents were. This is problematic for me. Everyone else is from some big city, from well-to-do homes, had ballet and piano lessons and many other things I had never heard about before. When I say that I'm from a village called Wereszczyn, that we weren't very well off, and that we had no servants, but a good grandmother who took care of me, I'm met with pity and scorn. I begin to be ashamed of my humble origins. My stories from home are about prayers on the Shabbat and holidays, about religious customs, and about my participation in all these. My stories don't make an impression on any of the children and I want to make an impression. As a result I decide to change my past and make a new impression. I must also be from a big city and a rich home. I adopt the city Lublin for this purpose. My late father conducted his commercial affairs in Lublin, and would tell me all kinds of stories about it. It was, therefore an easy place for me to adopt. I invent a completely imaginary story about my past, suitable to Lublin: very wealthy parents, a gigantic, well-furnished house, ballet and piano lessons and other things that the other children talked about. I didn't meet anyone at the orphanage who had come from a small village or a simple home like mine, therefore it was possible to invent any imaginary story. There's a Polish saying, "We used to have..." and it expresses the spirit of that period.

As soon as I left the orphanage I forgot all the stories I had made up about my past and was sorry I had behaved that way. I am very proud of my background, of my family and all the things I learned from them during the short time we had together. I carry wonderful childhood memories in my heart and wouldn't trade them for all the riches in the world. But, somehow, in the orphanage I had the feeling that if I didn't present myself as a big city girl from a rich family, the other children wouldn't accept me and might even taunt me about it, or that I would again become a second-rate child, as I was in the Bacher family.

Irka

In every place I've been ever since I lost my family, I've sought out someone to love, someone who would also return that love. So it was when I arrived at Helenuwek. I began to look for an object of my love. I am very fond of Heniek, who brought me here. I feel that he is a true friend and I am very attached to him, but the children interpret this friendship as a romance and secretly laugh at us. Their gossip makes me miserable and I look for a substitute for Heniek who could counteract the ridicule of the children.

There is a girl from the older group, called Irka, whom I like very much. I don't know whether she is aware of my distress or if she likes me as well. In any event, shortly after my arrival, we grow attached to one another and she takes me under her wing. Irka is four years older than I am. She's tall, pretty and bursting with health and optimism. She is always happy. She laughs and tells jokes. It's a great pleasure to be in her company. Many of the children adore her and want to be close to her. I am very proud of the fact that she has chosen to be my guardian. Over the course of time I grow so attached to her that I feel I can't live without her. I love her very much and she serves as a source of comfort for me, physically and emotionally. Irka takes care of me almost as a mother would. She washes and combs my hair, which has grown meanwhile. She hugs me when I'm upset, takes me for walks in the nearby forest, and sometime even to Lodz, and she defends me when I need defending. She's like an older sister, who does everything she can to make life more pleasant for me. Her attention strengthens the self-confidence, which I sorely lack. I learn from her to distinguish between important and trivial things, and not to aggravate myself over every comment the children make. She teaches me to take life more lightly than I'm accustomed. Our relationship lasted for many years, even after our paths parted. After parting, we sought each other out and always managed somehow to meet again.

The orphanage was a transitional station for most of us. Despite the fact that we are part of the People's Democratic Government of Poland, which is interested in educating us in the spirit of its ideology, we are secretly getting a Jewish and Zionist education, meant to lead us to immigrate to the Land of Israel. Polish law prohibits belonging to a Zionist movement, but it's in the orphanage that I learn, for the first time, about Zionism, the Land of Israel, and about the need for a Jewish State as the solution for the surviving refugees and the People of Israel. It is there that I learn songs about the longing for Zion in Yiddish and in Hebrew, and it is there that I learn the meaning of the prayer I had heard so many times in my home, *"Next year in Jerusalem".*

Most of the educators are deeply Zionist, members of the pioneering Youth Movements of the period before the war. While still in the forests and while fighting the Germans, they were planning the future of whoever would survive. Their sacred mission was to care for the Jewish children and youth. Wherever they were at the end of the Nazi occupation, they tried to find and gather Jewish children and youth, and to educate them towards immigrating to the Land of Israel, despite the danger entailed. The local survivors, previous members of the pioneering Zionist Youth movements, conduct all of the Zionist education we receive in Helenuwek in secret. I saw emissaries from the Land of Israel for the first time in the Displaced Persons camps in Germany. As far as I know, in 1945 these same youth movement members organized the transfer of the survivors from Poland to the areas occupied by the Allies. I think that the wondrous story of the organization of this transfer and the adventures connected with it, hasn't received the recognition it deserves in written history, despite the fact that it was a very important part of that period.

A Temporary Separation

In the summer of the year 1945 a rumor circulates in the orphanage that everyone above the age of sixteen will be permitted to leave the orphanage without the signature of an adult. According to the rumor, many of the members of the older group are planning to leave, but there are no visible signs of this, and on the surface everything remains as it was. The new school year is about to begin and the orphanage supplies all the older girls with new dresses made of the same cloth. Either accidentally or not, the cloth is blue and white. The atmosphere in the orphanage is one of beginning a new school year. However, something secret is going on in the older group. It's very mysterious and we, the younger children, aren't allowed to know about it. They get together in secret places, exchange secrets, make all sorts of preparations, but I have no idea why or what they're planning. Irka doesn't tell me anything, and I, don't pay much attention to what goes on in the older group. I live my day-to-day life so intensely, that I don't pay any attention to things that don't directly affect me.

When Irka comes one day to say 'good-bye', without any previous warning, I'm in shock. I burst out crying and ask her to take me with her and not to go anywhere without me. I cling to her with all my might and don't want to let her go. According to the agreement among those planning to leave, Irka is forbidden to tell me where she is going. However, when she sees how distraught I am, she decides to share the secret with me. She makes me swear never to reveal what she is about to tell me. She tells me that most of the older children are leaving the orphanage. They are leaving individually, but they intend to go as a group to the city of Czenstochow and to start a kibbutz, which will serve as their first station on the way to the Land of Israel. She gives me the address they are going to and tells me to come there if I miss her unbearably. There is some reassurance in what she tells me, making it easier for me to part from her.

The activities in the orphanage change after most of the older group leave. The only ones remaining in the older group are Communists and there are very few of them. They want to build a new world–here and now. The social activities undergo a dramatic change. There are no longer lectures about Judaism. Our joint activities with the senior group become few and far between. The joy and enthusiasm that had characterized life in the orphanage is dying out. This is possibly my subjective feeling because of Irka's absence. Everything has become dismal and meaningless for me. I'm so absorbed in my longing for her that I'm not capable of enjoying anything.

I don't know what a *kibbutz* is, and I don't know where Czenstochow is, and I don't know if the members of the *kibbutz* will accept me. It is enough that Irka is there, for me to decide to leave the orphanage which had barely agreed to have me, and for me to do everything I can to join Irka.

Running Away Again

During the first period of Irka's absence I try to overcome my sickly longing to be near her. My dependence on her frightens me. I understand that I can't always be with her. However, all my efforts to overcome this longing are in vain. When I feel that I can't bear it any longer, I decide to act. I tell no one about my true intentions, but I begin to spread a rumor among the children, that I'll be leaving the orphanage soon. Without thinking too much about the possible outcome, I go to the office and notify them that I want to leave Helenuwek. The answer I receive is that only at the age of sixteen and over, can anyone leave the orphanage on their own, and since I am only twelve years old, I will have to wait several years. If I want to leave in any event, I must bring the adult that I'll be living with, so that he can sign as my guardian.

Although it's very unpleasant for me to approach Roza again with a request for help, I know that the only possibility I have of obtaining guardianship is Roza. I don't know any other person I can turn to who would sign for me. I, therefore, go to Lodz with my new story. I tell Roza about Irka and the strong attachment between us and even reveal her secret about founding a *kibbutz* in Czenstochow, in order to convince her of the sincerity of my intentions, and of the importance of her signature. I ask her to come with me to Helenuwek and say that she is taking me home with her. I do this without caring that she will be incriminating herself by signing a false statement. I don't think about the results of my actions and their affect on others. I am selfish and care about nothing beyond my own wishes. I want to be free of the orphanage and any means of attaining that end are justified in my mind.

Roza is very uncertain about granting my request. She is worried about problems with the authorities, but my pleas are so insistent that she agrees in the end. One day Roza comes to Helenuwek, supposedly, in order to take me home with her. I don't say anything to any of the children as to why I am leaving and where I'm going. I pack my meager belongings, say good-bye to everyone and leave with Roza. Actually, we're going straight to the Lodz train station. She buys me a ticket to Czenstochow on the night train and she gives me some pocket money in case I need it. The parting between us is difficult for both of us. I have the feeling that perhaps we are now separating forever. She has no future plans connected to the Land of Israel, while within me the seed of Zionism is beginning to sprout. This is almost a final parting of our ways, and except for two meetings between us during her short visits to Israel, we never met again.

After Roza leaves, I realize that I am the only child among a great number of adults waiting for the night train. There is a very varied crowd, laden with many packages. It is the beginning of the winter of 1945, about half a year after the end of the war. Many people are still homeless, without any family and are wandering from place-to-place, seeking happiness. There are also many wandering peddlers with their goods. They are mainly farmers bringing their products to the big city. There was a great food shortage still then, and any edible food was immediately snatched up at exorbitant prices. The train station is very crowded and I'm lost in this mass of people like a lamb looking for its mother. I wait for the train like everyone else. Several people ask me why I am alone, if I can't find my parents, and if I need any help. I pretend that I'm perfectly all right and there is no need to worry about me. The truth of the matter is that I am very frightened both of riding on a train for the first time in my life, and of not being able to push myself onto the train. I have no idea what to do if I don't succeed in getting onto the train. I'm not prepared to approach Roza for help again and I have no other person I can turn to. When the train finally arrives, I forcefully push my way on like everyone else. I'm proud of myself and happy that I succeeded. I don't find a place to sit, but am thankful to find a place to stand in the aisle. A farmer's wife, sitting on the floor surrounded by baskets full of hens, feels sorry for me and invites me to sit beside her on her wide skirt. Her big body is pleasantly warm. The rumble of the wheels is monotonous and makes me drowsy. In a short time I fall into a deep sleep, which also releases me from finding false answers to questions about my destination, and why I am alone. At approximately two in the morning, the peasant woman wakes me and tells me that we've arrived at Czenstochow. I must get off the train. Outside it is very cold and very dark. It's hard for me to detach myself from the woman's body warmth, but this is no time to pamper myself. I gather my belongings, thank the peasant woman for her kindness and get off at the station.

Despite the masses of people around me, I feel a terrible loneliness. The people who got off the train begin to disperse in every direction. Some of them have people waiting for them. No one is waiting for me and I have no idea in which direction to go. Aside from the note with the address of Irka's *kibbutz,* I know nothing. The platform is already almost empty and I must also leave it. I come out to a cold and dark street and don't know what to do. I see a Russian soldier on one of the corners and decide to try getting help from him. I'm almost twelve years old, but look much younger. The soldier is very surprised to see me alone with no adult accompaniment. I show him the note with the address and ask him how I can get there. The soldier tells me that there is a night curfew. It is forbidden to be found in the streets now and those who disregard the curfew are severely punished. The soldier returns the note without even looking at it. I am so disappointed that I begin to cry. I succeeded in getting to Czenstochow without much difficulty, and now that I'm here and I'm so close, I'm stuck! I'm also freezing and very hungry, which makes me even more bitter and sorry for myself. I, evidentially, arouse the soldier's hidden feelings of compassion. I see that he is hesitant and doesn't send me away. I cry even harder in order to convince him to help me. I don't know what makes him accompany me. He takes the note in his hand and studies it carefully. He seems to be familiar with the street written on the note, since he takes my hand in his and we begin our journey to Garibaldi Street. It's cold and dark and it even snows a little. The streets are completely empty. We are the only people walking in the street; a Russian soldier wearing an army coat and carrying a Tommy Gun; holding the hand of a little Jewish girl carrying a small bundle. We walk along the desolate streets in the city of the Holy Virgin, looking for a street where a *kibbutz* of *Ha'Shomer Ha'Tzair* is being founded.

The long walk warms me up and the soldier's hand gives me a pleasant feeling of security. I suddenly feel that I don't want to be separated from him, I want our walk to go on and on. Just then the soldier stops, examines the note for the hundredth time and announces to the dim night, "Here it is". He leaves me alone opposite a locked gate and goes on his way without waiting for someone to come out and take me in. Again, I am alone, standing before a locked gate. I shout and bang on the gate with my fists, but nothing happens. When I despair of anyone coming to the gate, I curl up, exhausted, in one of the corners and wait for morning. I don't dare move, even to pee, because of the curfew. In the end I am overcome by exhaustion and fall into a deep sleep filled with dreams.

On the Road

A Minor in the Kibbutz

I wake up to the sound of laughter. Some of the members of *Kibbutz Tzcenstohov* find me sleeping next to the gate that was opened in the morning. Since no one knows about my arrival, including Irka, they are very surprised to find me there. The first question they ask me isn't how and why I came, but whether Franush from the orphanage will also be coming to the *kibbutz*. I didn't understand then that it was a provocative question meant to mock me. Franush was the youngest child in the orphanage, perhaps three or four years old, and they who are over sixteen feel very adult and are ridiculing my surprise arrival at their *kibbutz* without any previous request for permission to do so. They don't consider me fitting for their pace of life. I understood the biting insults of their reception only later, when I matured a bit. I am so absorbed in my desire to be with Irka that nothing else has any meaning to me. Despite how sensitive I am to how other people relate to me, I don't understand that many of the *kibbutz* members have reservations about my coming there. The moment Irka appears I embrace her and cover her with kisses, forgetting all my problems, and my world becomes warm and secure. Imagine that my sudden arrival caused her a great deal of embarrassment, but my mind wasn't occupied with that. I have the feeling that I did the right thing at the right time. When I'm asked why I came to the *kibbutz,* I tell the truth and shamelessly declare to them all that I want to be near Irka, and that's why I'm here.

Life in the *Ha'Shomer Ha'Tzair kibbutz* in Czenstochow appears to me like living on a chessboard. Each one of the girls and boys has their own square. Each one has a clearly defined task. The organization of life here is different from every other way of life with which I was acquainted until now. There are committees, someone in charge of the work roster, and office and managerial work. There are people responsible for the connection with the outside world and those who are responsible for solving internal problems. It is a small, organized world, where everyone knows exactly his or her place.

They don't know where to place me in the jigsaw puzzle of their life. It takes quite a long time for me to find my place and become one of them. It's a very uncomfortable situation. Everyone in the *kibbutz* works, though I have a hard time finding a suitable place to work. Finally, I find a place that gives me a feeling of satisfaction. I was an expert at peeling potatoes when I worked on the Grabnik Estate, and since we ourselves cook the food we eat, I peel everything that needs to be peeled. I'm very proud that I can make myself useful and work like all the grown-up members. In addition to work, there are many discussions about principles and values and also many communal social activities. I don't understand much in the discussions, nevertheless, I don't miss any of them, in order to make the impression that I'm involved in what's happening and understand what's being discussed. On the whole, I feel good. The members learn to love me and accept me for what I am.

I don't remember how many people were in the *kibbutz,* but I do remember that it was very crowded. Since there wasn't enough room for a bed for each person, the beds were built on two levels, but even then there was a lack of beds, so in many cases people slept two in a bed. Usually a fat person was placed with a thin one. I shared a bed with a young girl called *Tova*, whom I didn't know from the orphanage. *Tova* was a big, chubby girl, older than most of the *kibbutz* members. I don't know how she came to the *kibbutz* and she didn't remain with us all the way. She had a motherly look and a full body that radiated warmth and softness. The beds are narrow, too narrow even for one person. For two people they are very crowded. As a result our bodies were intertwined with one another when we slept and *Towa's* embrace sometimes reminded me of my mother's embrace, which I've been longing for all these years. I didn't meet *Tova* again after we left Czenstochow. However, several years after my arrival in Israel, I learned that she had joined a *Kibbutz* belonging to the youth movement *Dror* (Freedom), and had been among the founders of *Kibbutz Lohamey Ha'Getaot* (Kibbutz of the Ghetto Fighters). Despite the fact that we were together for a relatively short time, she still has a warm place in my heart, among the human pantheon I remember from those days.

Irka is my guardian during my entire stay in Czenstochow, and I share all my burdens and all my joys with her. One of the first things we do together in the *kibbutz* is to take a walk through the Czenstochow market. When I am more acclimatized to the *kibbutz*, Irka asks me secretly if I have any money. She explains that it isn't worthwhile to tell anyone that I have money, because the *kibbutz* will take it from me and put it in the common treasury, and I, personally won't be able to use it. She suggests that we enjoy it secretly together. I have some money that Roza gave me, and I gladly agree to Irka's proposal. I am certain that all her suggestions are wise. One day we slip away from the *kibbutz* and go to the Czenstochow Market with my money. There isn't a great choice of products there. Only eight months have passed since the end of the war and there are shortages of everything. I don't remember all the things we bought there, but I clearly remember the bunch of grapes we bought. The grapes were wondrously juicy, and I savored the heavenly taste for as long as I could. We sat on a tree stump at the edge of the market. I was happy to take part in our thrilling, secret adventure. I spent all my meager savings and had no regrets whatsoever. I felt we had done something very special and I was grateful to Irka for showing me how it's possible to outsmart an entire *kibbutz.*

Along with the daily routine of the *kibbutz*, vigorous secret preparations are being made for illegally leaving Poland. One day a gigantic notice appears on the bulletin board, announcing a very important, closed meeting of the *kibbutz*, which everyone is obliged to attend. An important guest comes to the meeting. I learn afterwards that he is active in organizing the escape from

Poland. The doors are closed from the inside and our guest tells us that he has come to prepare us for the escape. The only way we can leave Poland is as Greek Jews returning to their homeland. We will have to learn the Greek language and temporarily forget the other languages we know. Our exit from Poland is secret, and there are many hostile elements that will attempt to impede us. They will try in various ways to discover our true identity. We must, therefore, be very cautious in what we say. One person's mistake can lead to the arrest of us all, or even to exile in Siberia. His words terrify me to the point that I feel constantly tense, until we actually leave Poland. I am afraid that I won't be able to withstand the inspections at the border, because I don't know how to lie.

A Greek from Saloniki

Since we are supposed to leave Poland as Greek Jews returning to their homeland, we each receive a Greek Jewish name. My new name is Sarizi Miriam. We are taught how to say *"Good morning"* and *"Good night"* in Greek. We are supposed to say that we are Greek Jews from Saloniki, who were deported by the Germans to concentration camps in Poland, and we are now returning home. It is forbidden for us to say a word in Polish or Yiddish in the presence of strangers. We are permitted to speak Hebrew, but none of us knows Hebrew. Most of us had heard the Holy language at home when our parents prayed, but we don't understand a word of the language and are unable to converse in it. Actually, we're forbidden to speak at all from the moment we set foot on the train in Czenstochow going to the border between Poland and Czechoslovakia. I'm extremely tense. I'm afraid I'll suddenly say a word in Polish, thereby incriminating myself and everybody else. When we arrive at the border post, the border police must inspect us personally. Outside there are many Russian soldiers armed with Tommy guns, and inside the checkpoint cabin there are Polish policemen and policewomen. I feel paralyzed with fear before the inspection. When I enter the cabin, a Polish policewoman looks at me suspiciously and says sarcastically, "You don't look Greek at all. One can see from your eyes and your nose that you're a native of Poland". I think she has discovered my true identity and that this is the end of my journey, but the show goes on. I pretend that I'm stupid and don't understand what's wanted of me. Instead of doing what she tells me to do, I very slowly do the opposite of almost everything. My slow reactions to her instructions irritate her and in the end she is glad to get rid of me, because I was holding up her work and there was a long line of people waiting.

When I go outside, I am praised by Bella, my leader. She had seen what pressure I was under before the inspection, and despite the fact that she didn't witness what happened inside, she is proud that I succeeded in passing the inspection without revealing my identity. The Russian soldiers, who are very curious about us and perhaps suspicious as well, ask us many questions. We had been instructed not to answer any questions, but to direct the curious soldiers to our leaders. I remember one of the questions to this day. A Russian soldier asked one of the boys, what his Tommy gun is called in Greek. The boy, who was somewhat confused and frightened, pretends that he doesn't understand the question and sends the soldier to our leader, Bella. The Russian soldier doesn't unnerve Bella, who has been accompanying us all the way, even in the orphanage, and who was a partisan during the war. When she understands the question, she answers without hesitation, that in Greek a Tommy gun is called, *"Avtmat"*. We all tensely await the soldier's response. Perhaps he understands Greek and is trying to trip us up. Fortunately for us, the soldier is satisfied with the answer and doesn't ask any further questions. I don't know how much was paid to whom, but I have no doubt that otherwise we wouldn't have succeeded in crossing the border with such ease. With the conclusion of the inspection at the Polish Border, we board the train to Czechoslovakia. From there we will have to cross the border to Germany illegally.

Repatriation

The moment we leave Poland we must again change our identities. We become Jewish refugees, from Germany, returning home. We are called German repatriates. I again take on a different name. From Sarizi Miriam, the Greek, I become Johanna Heller, a sixty year-old native of Germany. Our leaders keep our documents in order to hide the falsifications. We are on a train headed for Czechoslovakia. I am leaving the borders of Poland for the first time in my life. My life is changing at such a rapid pace now, that I can't really absorb what's happening around me.

Czechoslovakia! A foreign country! New people and landscapes. Nothing is familiar. The sights passing by outside the windows are also unfamiliar and my curiosity grows from minute to minute, with each forward movement. I had never seen mountains before. I knew of their existence from stories and songs, but not in reality. When we come to a place where the train travels between the mountains, and even through a tunnel carved into the mountain, I'm enchanted by the sight. Despite the fact that many other things occupy my mind the mountainous landscape opening up before me is overwhelming.

We are all completely exhausted. The tension of crossing the Polish border was very tiring and that was just the beginning of our journey. We don't know what to expect, and we're anxious about the future. Leaving Poland, where I was born and where I experienced all the horrors of the war, is the first step in our journey to the Land of Israel and it is already behind us. Will the rest of the way go as smoothly? Mixed feelings. It's very hard for me to leave Poland, although I don't want to continue living there. I have the feeling that something very essential has been torn away from me. I am abandoning, perhaps forever, my happy childhood years, my home and my family's communal grave. Am I doing the right thing? Are the dead angry with me for deserting them? How will I keep my oath if I won't ever be able to return to Poland? Tears come to my eyes. "Goodbye, my beloved- hateful country. There is no way now to return to you". Our leaders tell us that we are on our way to a new life, and that we must go on, without looking back.

We spend many days on the Czech train without a place to sleep, without a place to wash up and without organized meals, but we don't complain. We sleep sitting up. Sometimes we put our heads on our neighbor's lap and sleep a little better. We are very careful not to utter any Polish words in our sleep. Since there are Russian soldiers in every car, our leaders arrange guard duty to assure that no one shouts anything in his mother tongue while sleeping. The train is very crowded, and we are the youngest of the travelers.

I don't remember how long the journey was, but I do remember that food was very limited, and we would eat in our seats on the moving train. Actually we spent that entire journey sitting on forty square centimeters of a bench. From time to time we get off at one of the stations to breathe some fresh air and to stretch our legs. We have to be careful not to get lost in the masses of people spilling out of the train and rushing back inside. Our first destination is the city Bratislava.

We arrive in Bratislava at two o'clock in the morning and walk from the station to the hotel where we spend the night. The name of the hotel is *"Hotel Yelen"* and it is full of refugees like us passing through. To this day I remember the echo of our steps at night in the Bratislava streets, paved with rectangular bricks. I had never seen such bricks in Poland and they made a great impression on me. I have the feeling that I am part of some game, a cube being pushed along in all directions on a board of rectangular bricks. Sometimes I enjoy the game and at other times I grow tired of it. I can't stop the game when I want to, because I am attached to many other cubes that preserve the game, and I am obliged to continue – despite my fatigue. Eventually, after an endless and exhausting night march, the board of rectangular bricks comes to an end, and we halt beside *Hotel Yelen*. We are led into a very large room, the floor of which is covered with a blanket of straw. I immediately collapse onto the straw as though it were a royal bed. I don't hear the leaders' instructions and I don't notice who is next to me. I fall asleep the moment I lie down on the straw and nothing has the power to disturb me.

The only sight in Bratislava that has been engraved in my memory is the streets paved in a pattern of rectangular bricks. All else has been completely forgotten. Bratislava is a station of transition in our long journey from Poland to Germany. Only a short time after our arrival we leave for the train that will bring us to beautiful Prague and after that, to Carlsbad.

An Unexpected Sandwich

The train ride to Prague follows the same routine as that from Poland to Bratislava. It is a little less crowded, and the people look more elegant. Only our modest menu doesn't change and we are hungry most of the time. We have no cooked food during the entire journey, and even the bread, which is our daily food, is strictly rationed. Food shortages carried over from the war days, are still prevalent and even money can't buy sufficient food. The refugees aren't the only ones who suffer from hunger. The entire local population hungers for food. Personal hygiene is also a problem for us. I remember wearing the same dress all through the journey, taking no showers and practically never combing my hair. I had a kind of army coat with silver buttons and a thin flowery dress, which were immortalized in the photo on my immigration certificate. I haven't changed my clothes and I'm filthy, neglected and stinky. Most of my companions are in the same situation as me, which is some small consolation. The local population looks entirely different. They're clean and well dressed. Compared to us, some of them even wear luxurious clothes.

One day an especially well-dressed man gets on the train. He is wearing a long, grey coat and a matching hat, well-pressed trousers with a crease in the front, and shiny black shoes. He looks like a movie star and attracts everyone's attention. The man sits next to us and looks at us with obvious curiosity for a long time. We begin to suspect that he is a detective who is trying to deduce who we are. I don't know why, but suddenly he gestures to me to come to him. I don't know what he wants of me and I am afraid to approach him. I'm afraid he will ask me questions that I am forbidden to answer, and I won't know how to handle the situation. We are extremely aware of the fact that a mistake made by one of us can put us all under suspicion. However, the man insists. Having no choice, I unwillingly approach him, blushing from shame and fear. When I reach him, I lower my eyes and wait. The man doesn't speak to me, just looks at me with admiring eyes and waits for me to relax a little. When he sees that I am a little more at ease, he takes a sandwich wrapped in wax paper out of his pocket and hands it to me. In order not to make the others jealous and not to embarrass me, he opens his elegant coat to hide me from the other children. He insists that I eat the sandwich immediately and don't try to share it. The sandwich consists of two slices of fresh black bread smeared with homemade raspberry jam. Its taste is outstanding, divine. Perhaps this is due to the circumstances, or to the shortage of food, or perhaps it was actually delicious. To this day, I remember that taste well. I don't know why that man decided to give up his meal, or why he chose me to give it to. In my opinion, there was nothing about me that could attract attention. I was dirty, uncombed and smelled from neglect, while he was so elegant. I was amazed that not only wasn't he repulsed by me, but even put me on his lap. I have not met with such a humane gesture since the end of the war. I enjoy eating the sandwich and tears run down my cheeks. The man waits patiently until I swallow the last bite and without saying a word, he releases me from his warm lap.

On that day the Czech people won a special place in my heart. I don't know who the man was, or his name, or what motivated him to do what he did. We didn't converse at all, but the sandwich he offered me in his unique way, has remained an unforgettable, wonderful memory.

Forgotten in the Hammock

Our journey continued for endless days and nights without any intermediate stations and our fatigue became unbearable. Each one of us tries to get a few winks of sleep each day and barely succeeds in doing so. I am on the verge of collapse. I get dizzy and lose my balance. The leaders try to find me a more comfortable place than the bench, so that I can sleep more and gain my strength back. On the last night before arriving in Prague they arrange a bed for me in the hammock above the seat. This is a regal bed compared to sleeping on the bench. There are no neighbors on either side whose heads fall on your shoulder from time to time and wake you up. The bed is soft and it's possible to get a good night's sleep there.

When I open my eyes, there is complete silence all around. The coach is empty and the train isn't moving. I don't know where I am and why I am alone. I become very frightened. Did they forget me in the hammock!? They left without me and I'm alone again?! I feel as lost as I've ever felt in my worst moments. Without a language, or some kind of identification, a German refugee returning to her homeland, who doesn't know German, who doesn't know from where and to which cities she is traveling. What should I do? Who can I turn to? I jump out of my comfortable bed and rush outside. I see a gigantic and beautiful station with many platforms, masses of people moving in all directions, but my companions aren't among them. Where should I go? I burst out crying and can't stop. I am certain that they didn't notice my absence and continued without me. I run from platform to platform in a panic trying to find the group. Luckily, no one stops me or pays any attention to me while I'm running about. If that were to happen, then I would have really been in trouble. After I had been running about endlessly, or at least so it appeared to me, I finally find the group sitting comfortably in one of the corners of the station, waiting for the leaders who are arranging the continuation of our journey.

I feel deeply wounded by this incident. No one is relieved by my return, just as no one was upset by my absence. To this day I don't know if they were aware of my absence or not, or if they bothered to look for me at all. It was a frightful trauma for me, but the others in the group just joked about it. In any event, during the rest of the journey, I didn't agree to any suggestions that I sleep in the baggage hammock, despite the fact that sleeping there was comparatively comfortable and we continued to travel by train until we arrived in Germany.

We spend about three days in the capital of Czechoslovakia, Prague. As opposed to most Polish cities that I have seen, Prague wasn't destroyed at all during the war, and there are no signs of bombing and shelling. I know almost nothing about the city, although I heard the name when my father discussed the German conquest of Prague with his Polish neighbors. I also heard the story about the *Golem of Prague* spoken about at home, but I never expected to ever be there. I'm very curious about the *Golem,* although I'm also afraid of him. When we walk through the streets of Prague, I expect to meet him in one of the narrow alleyways, hoping that he won't hurt me of course. When we visit the Jewish cemetery, I find the ancient gravestones sad, and also exciting. I study each gravestone with curiosity and envy. Each person has a name and some indication of his past life. I have only a mass grave holding 320 Jews, with no gravestone, and no epitaph to indicate that they once existed. Actually, only my memories, and my physical existence serve as my family's gravestone.

This city is so beautiful that even people absorbed in their own affairs, as I am, cannot remain indifferent towards it. For three weeks we've been walking back and forth in the streets and they are so stunning that one never tires of them. I'm astonished by the multitude of gorgeous palaces that are particularly impressive at night when they are lit up from the outside. I never imagined that there were so many in the entire world, and certainly not in one single city. Prague is magical to me and not at all real. I feel that

I am wandering for days on end in the world of fairy tales. Never before have I seen anything so splendid. Prague captures my heart. We walk on the Charles Bridge and its surroundings. I'm entranced by the statues at the sides of the bridge. I didn't think it was possible to represent people and animals so precisely. I look into the flowing water of the river under the bridge and at the reflections of the palaces in the water. I don't want to leave this beautiful bridge.

I haven't seen Prague since then, but when I close my eyes, I can see it in my imagination even today. I don't remember where we stayed and where we ate, but I remember the great impression the city's beauty made on me. Everything we managed to see and to experience there was a wonderful gift bestowed on us. Nevertheless, most important thing to us at that time was the continuation of our journey – each step of which brought us closer to the Land of Israel. We, therefore, were happy when we boarded the train to Carlsbad and felt no remorse at leaving the lovely city.

Welcome to Carlsbad

We have the same routine on the way from Prague to Carlsbad that we had up to then: riding in a train day and night, in a limited space, with very little to eat. We become accustomed to life on the train and I almost forget that it's possible to live, and especially to sleep, without the jolting of the coach and the rumbling of the wheels. Sometime I imagine that I am in the cradle I slept in when I was three years old, and the shaking of the coach is the rocking of the cradle. Ever since we left Poland, we've been traveling on the rails of Czechoslovakia and we are now nearing the end. The last train station in this country is the train station in Carlsbad. The train stops at quite a late hour and immediately masses of Russian soldiers get on in order to examine the documents of the passengers, and of course, our documents, as well. This is a border station and the inspections are thorough and lengthy. We are not allowed to disembark from the train and a rumor is spread that we are under arrest. The Russian soldiers discard our documents (held together by our leaders), on suspicion of fraud. Our leaders disappear with our documents and we anxiously await their return, so as to have some information about the continuation of our journey. However, not one of them returns.

At approximately midnight, we are told to get off the train, to arrange ourselves in rows of three and to begin to walk. We are accompanied by Russian soldiers. Our leaders were taken to the authorities and there is no one to keep us informed about what's happening or to show us how to behave in the given situation. Not one of us knows where we are being taken or what will happen to us. We obey instructions, since we are now surrounded by Russian soldiers, and any attempt to refuse to obey an order would complicate the situation even more. Nevertheless, there are those among us who suggest that we refuse. Our midnight walk through the streets of Carlsbad goes on without end and we are convinced that we are being taken to some kind of prison, and then what will happen? Surprisingly, the soldiers stop before a lavish hotel and tell us to go inside. The older children among us say that we shouldn't go in. They suspect that it is a trap, but the soldiers insist upon it and we obey. The moment we are inside the hotel, the soldiers leave us to our fate.

Another surprise awaits us in the hotel. We are greeted as guests in every way. We are taken to our rooms and each one of us has his own bed covered with white bedding and a large towel. In each room there is a bathtub with tiled walls, gold faucets, fragrant soap and hot and cold water. Unbelievable! Many of us have never seen such things ever since we lost our homes. We don't know what to do in this situation.

The tension we felt since our leaders were arrested and our midnight walk to some unknown destination, vanishes all at once. There are no longer any constraints, no Russian soldiers guarding us, and also no leaders to give us instructions, or to restrain our behavior. Instead of that, there is total freedom and lavishly furnished rooms as in a palace. The surprise is so staggering that in our joy and confusion we go wild. We run from room to room, throw things at one another. Pillows fly in the air as though they are balls to play with. The towels also become toys to be thrown from one to the other. Some children go into the bathtubs in their clothes to see if they're the right size. Others jump on the beds as they would on a trampoline. It becomes an out of control rampage. Many of us join hands to make a long line and dance from room to room, singing loudly. The hotel staff is helpless in the face of this rampage. They find no way of calming us down. The frenzy continues until the following morning. Most of us fall asleep in various corners, in weird positions, and not in the beds that are waiting for us. When the leaders arrive in the morning, they are stunned by the mess. Fortunately for us, they are able to placate the hotel management and to settle the issue amicably.

I am in a daze. This is the first time that I have been in a hotel, and I am overwhelmed by its splendor. It's the first time I've ever seen a bathtub and I have to be taught how to use it. The golden faucets, the magnificent furniture, the carvings in the furniture – seem to be part of a dream that I'm floating in, like "Alice in Wonderland". Our leaders inform us that we will remain in the hotel until our documents are returned, which will probably be in another few days. In the meantime they try to organize pleasant activities for us. Today, I understand that our vacation week in the lovely spa city Carlsbad and the legalizing of our documents must have cost a great deal of money. Someone probably knows how that money was obtained and from what source, but that information was never revealed to me.

I have wonderful memories of our time spent in Carlsbad, despite all the complications. Like all European countries after the war, Czechoslovakia suffers from a shortage of food and is obliged to distribute food by means of rationing coupons. One coupon can buy a plate of watery soup with some potatoes floating in the liquid. On the other hand, high quality beer is almost free. We don't eat much, but we all drink beer – even the youngest among us. The beer tastes bitter, but it fills our empty stomachs and improves our morale. I remember myself, and all those around me, being intoxicated all the time. Our daily schedule in Carlsbad is very full. We walk through the city, visit the hot springs – but we don't bathe in them. We take walks in the surrounding woods and every day we find ourselves in another enchanting spot in the city. Someone looking at us from outside probably sees a strange sight: a large group of raggedly dressed young people and children, drunkenly touring through all the tourist sights– a strange brand of 'end of the war' tourists. However, while we are enjoying ourselves, someone is working hard to retrieve our documents and to prepare the continuation of our journey. I don't remember the name of the beautiful hotel we stayed in, or what exactly we saw in the city, but at the age of twelve I became a confirmed beer drinker due to that week in Carlsbad.

After almost a week of drunken elation, we are informed that the authorities have certified our documents and now we must prepare to illicitly cross the border to our next destination, Germany, where the Allies are in control.

Between Two Worlds

Crossing the border from countries under Russian jurisdiction to countries under Allied jurisdiction must be conducted secretly. One of the passage points between the Russian sector and the American sector is located under the bridge on the outskirts of Carlsbad. The border is in the middle of the bridge and is guarded by soldiers from both armies. The soldiers change shifts every few hours and our secret passage under the bridge is to be carried out at the midnight change of the guard. We must wait for a dark and misty night to carry out this operation successfully. There is a hiding place a short distance before the bridge. We wait there for permission, from those in charge of the operation, to start moving secretly in the direction of the free world. We are in a gigantic pit hidden from sight, but exposed to the rain and snow. It's cold and dark there, but it assures us we won't be discovered. We are obliged to spend hours there, and it reminds me of the bunker that I sat in during the war.

The person in charge of our group's passage under the bridge is a young Jew called Moshe Laufer, who is intimately familiar with all the secret escape routes in the area. He knows every path and each stone on the way, and he is the one who decides when it's possible, and when it's impossible to cross the border. Everything is conducted in accordance with his instructions. He returns us to the hiding place under the bridge three times during that week. We wait in dead silence. Every little noise, every suspicious movement might thwart our entire operation, and could even cause the loss of lives. I don't know what the reasons are for returning us to the hotel twice. The reasons are probably justified. Although I enjoy the time spent in Carlsbad, it's a disappointment to return to the hotel. I have no idea how we manage to keep our rooms at the hotel. They seem to be at our disposal at any time. We leave during the evening and return the same night without any problem. I imagine that in this case as well, everything was accomplished with the help of large sums of money.

Those nights of waiting, before our escape from Czechoslovakia, have been indelibly engraved in my memory, and even left me an enduring souvenir. I came down with a severe case of pneumonia, from lying in the snow. I didn't receive any medical treatment, since I didn't have a bad cough and I didn't complain. I imagine that even if I had complained it wouldn't have made any difference. The leaders were so occupied with issues of crossing the border that they were incapable of paying attention to minor issues, like health. Two attempts to cross the border at night concluded by returning to the hotel. However, on the third attempt we were not returned to Carlsbad.

During the third night of hiding in the pit, (as in all the previous nights), we lie quietly waiting for the signal to move. Close to midnight we receive instructions to get up without making any noise. Moshe Laufer instructs us to hold hands and form a single line behind him. He has a square light-colored patch sewn on to his back which can easily be seen by the person behind him. These are precautions to prevent anyone from getting lost. This handholding chain consists of approximately one hundred children and youth, who recently experienced the horrors of war, and know that their lives are dependent on a quiet and successful passage under the bridge. When the ruckus of changing the guard begins, we are located exactly in front of the entrance beneath the bridge. It is a dark and freezing night. Our vision is blurred by the falling snow, and we can barely distinguish who is walking in front of us and holding our hand. We hear the shouts of the guards, a mixture of languages which sounds like howling in the quiet night. The steps of the guards walking on the bridge echo loudly and sound to us like rolling thunder. Our long human chain must manage to cross to the other side of the bridge before the soldiers finish changing shifts. It is a quiet, rapid and difficult walk. I don't know whether I tremble because of the tension of the situation, or because of fever from pneumonia. This walk is unbearably difficult for me and I feel that I won't hold on to the end. I trip a few times, but fortunately I'm small and thin, and my neighbors to the left and to the right can drag me along until I regain my balance. I don't know how far we must walk, but to me it seems endless. We continue to walk for about two hours on forest paths and through bushes and thickets, until we come to an isolated train station in a clearing of the forest. I feel as though I have no strength left in me.

In retrospect, I think the organization that arranged the escape undertook a mission upon itself, and upon the children that was too difficult, too dangerous, and almost beyond our ability to carry out. However, the organizers also displayed great courage, and faith in our stamina. I think that only children like us, who had experienced what we had experienced in our short lives, could have endured such hardships. I'm not at all sure that children leading normal lives could have born the hardships we were called upon to bear.

The train station we arrive at that night is already in German territory. A freight train used for transporting coal is waiting for us and that's where we sleep the rest of the night, after our exhausting struggles. We are so tired that we don't even pay attention to the fact that we are already in the Allied Zone. We also pay no attention to the filth we are lying in. We fall asleep immediately. When we leave the train in the morning, we don't recognize one another. It is an extremely funny sight:

The world around us is sparkling clean, after the snow that fell during the night, while we are black as Negroes from the coal dust in the train. Looking at one another, we are overcome with laughter and begin to wash ourselves with snow, while throwing snowballs at one another. Many of us roll in the snow and become uncontrollably wild again – like at a merry Purim party. We are happy and very proud of ourselves for succeeding in escaping to the Free World with almost no mishaps. Not one of us collapsed along the way. Even I, who feel so sick, am proud of myself for holding on and not causing any delays.

Sixty Year Old Johanna Heller

Here I am, still Johanna Heller returning to her homeland, Germany. I am again on a train, this time, a German train bringing my friends and I to the city of Munich. Since my liberation by the Red Army, I haven't encountered any Germans, nor have I heard their language. Suddenly I'm again surrounded by Germans and I hear the language used to give commands that brought about the loss of millions of people and the annihilation of European Jewry – among them, my entire family. I see every German as my personal enemy, who participated or aided in the murder of my family. I want revenge. I want to do something bad to them, to humiliate them, but I don't know how. I am not the only one who feels that way. All of us feel the need for revenge, and feel that it is our moral obligation. We plan all sorts of cruel revenge, but we can't really do anything. The most severe revenge that most of my friends discover is to spit in their faces. I'm not capable of doing that. I don't dare, some inner sense stops me. There are also those who express their need for revenge by cursing the

Germans in the train, with the worst curses they know. Others let elderly Germans stand and don't offer them a seat even when they demand it. The time has finally come when a Jewish child can humiliate the masters of the world with impunity. This affords us some satisfaction and pride.

The truth of the matter is that the Germans crowded in the train look neglected and shabbily clothed, and don't at all resemble the lords of the country, as I imagined them all during the war. There is no hint of the order and cleanliness the Germans take such pride in. If they weren't Germans, I would have pitied some of them. I, too, am preoccupied during most of the train ride with thoughts about my private revenge. When I don't succeed in thinking of anything original, I decide to do what many of my friends are doing. I refuse to offer my seat to the elderly Germans, in spite of their demands. I don't know how to hate, even Germans, and I'm not pleased with my behavior. My conscience bothers me, but I don't succumb to it. I decide that I will obey the teachings from my home, "to rise before the elderly" when it concerns other people, and not the Germans.

In the Munich train station there is much commotion and confusion. A jumble of different languages and raggedly dressed people hurry in every direction. Within this mass of people there is a group of religious American Jews wandering about. They are dressed in the traditional attire of religious Jews including *Kapotas* (black satin overcoats) and fur hats, which we called *'Shtreimel'.* They resemble the *'Hasidim'* in my village, and I am amazed to see them here, in Germany. I don't know how they were informed of our arrival in Munich, but they're part of our welcoming committee and they try to convince us to go with them to America. Two Talmudic students approach me and begin to speak to me in Yiddish. They speak exactly as we spoke at home. They very gently ask me what happened to me during the war and I am deeply moved by this meeting with them. They remind me of people I've known and thought no longer existed after the 'final solution'.

After a series of questions they start to persuade me to come to America with them and they promise me 'paradise on earth'. In America I will want for nothing, they assure me that they will provide me with a good religious home. They promise me a groom, a wedding and a dowry. I listen politely to all the promises, but categorically refuse to go to America. If they offered to bring me up in the Land of Israel as a religious Jewess, I might agree, but I don't agree to give up the idea of Israel. I am already a deeply committed Zionist. I know exactly what I want. Although I'm only twelve years old, I already have an independent outlook on life, and I am not prepared to go to America under any circumstances. I don't know how long the Americans spent trying to persuade us, but they didn't succeed in persuading anyone in our group. The leaders kept an eye on what was going on, but there was no need for their intervention.

After the leaders manage to make our sleeping arrangements for the night, they collect us up from the midst of the bustle and take us for a tour of the streets of devastated Munich. They take us to the museum that Hitler declared would be the only place where Jews would remain, as a museum exhibit, after he won the war. This museum serves as temporary living quarters for Jewish survivors who somehow found their way to Germany. Here, the various groups are registered and screened before being sent to Displaced Persons (DP) Camps. To this day I don't know if the museum was chosen as a hostel for survivors because it wasn't completely destroyed by the bombings of the Allied Forces, or as a symbol of our survival and as undeniable proof of Hitler's failure to annihilate the Jewish people.

Displaced Persons

Flimsy Partitions

The passage from Munich to the Displaced Persons Camp in Fernwald is vague in my memory, but I remember the place itself very well. In the eyes of a child who believed that almost no Jews had been left alive in Europe after the war, the number of Jews located in Fernwald seems enormous. We, along with most of the other survivors are lodged in long buildings with round roofs, evidently military structures, made available for us. These buildings are very long with no rooms or partitions. Each family unit or individual is allotted several meters of space. Sheets and blankets serve as partitions between the residents' allotted areas.

It's impossible to have any privacy, however, having no choice; people manage to lead comparatively normal lives between those flimsy partitions. Couples have sexual intercourse, babies are born, families celebrate their special occasions, and friends get together to talk. The survivors try to live as fully as possible under those circumstances. Still, at times, all the residents of the long building are awakened at night by the screams of those who are reliving the horror of the past in their dreams. I envy every family unit I encounter. I long for the warmth of a home, for a loving family and, above all, I long to belong to someone. I feel like Heidi's song: "I'm alone like a stone". The fact that there is no one in the world, who is acquainted with my family or my background, hurts me deeply. The substitutes for my family are the children my age who live with me in the various stations of my wanderings. There are those whom I still feel attached to as though they were family.

The various *Halutzic* (pioneer) movements in Fernwald try to prepare the youth affiliated with them for a long stay in the camp. No one knows when our turn will come to go to the Land of Israel. *Kibbutzim* are set up. These *kibbutzim* are made up of groups of youngsters – of the same age – who are expected to independently organize and run their collective lives. A *kibbutz* somewhat resembles the training farms of the period before the war. I, too, belong to such a *kibbutz* and our leaders help us get organized and become independent. We're very proud that at our age we are capable of living independently, without the aid of adults. We cook for ourselves, wash our own laundry, and clean the house. We have elected committees who manage all the aspects of our life together. We, the members of *Ha'Shomer Ha'Tzair,* who strongly believe in our mission, are getting a preview of *kibbutz* life. We are dressed in uniforms made of the stiff canvas material of tents. We wear the *Shomer* blue tie and look like real scouts. We march through the streets of the camp singing ardent marching songs in Yiddish and in Hebrew – without understanding the meaning of the words. We're doing everything we can to prepare ourselves for life in the Land of Israel, and are impatiently waiting for our departure. We tirelessly dance the *Horah* because we are told it is an Israeli dance. We want to be Israeli in every way. There is a Russian circle dance called *"Tzitzutka"*, in which the speed of the dancing increases all the time. Very few people are able to keep dancing to the end of the accompanying music. Despite the fact that I am among the youngest dancers, I always succeed in remaining until the end of the dance and I am very proud of myself.

In addition, there is a rich social and cultural life in Fernwald. We have a "mini" Zionist Jewish State there with *kibbutzim* of all the various youth movements. Sometimes the disputes are so fervent that they develop into fistfights. There is also a Jewish theatre that produces many plays, affording me the opportunity of seeing theatre for the first time in my life. The plays that I see transport me into a reality, different from my daily existence and I find it enthralling each time.

In Fernwald meet people from the land of Israel for the first time. There are two emissaries from "the land" and the encounter with them is incredibly emotional, the meeting had a holy atmosphere, and was exhilarating. Each one of us wants to touch them, in order to sense the land of Israel through them. They are members of *Kibbutz Yakum*. The man is named Israel and the girl, *Yona*. She teaches us a popular Hebrew song called "Our Little Homeland", and translates the words into Yiddish for us. That song is the essence of how I imagine our homeland to be, and I continue to sing it for days on end. Here we also meet soldiers from the Jewish Brigade for the first time. The sight of

Jews in uniform is absolutely exhilarating. We, who experienced so much humiliation, who had no means of defending ourselves, see the Brigade soldiers as the redeeming army of the Jewish people, who will also defend us when necessary.

Most of our time is spent learning about Zionism and Socialism. The leaders are trying to make good Jews of us and to develop in us a concern for all humanity, and not only for ourselves. I don't really understand why I should care about all of humanity. After all, humanity didn't worry about me when I was persecuted by the Nazis. I also don't understand exactly why there are so many youth movements and why there is so much controversy among them. We all long to go to the same beloved country. We all dream about a just world. So, where is the argument? The administration of the camp takes pride in the fact that it succeeded in creating nearly normal lives for the survivors in very abnormal conditions. Actually, the entire Jewish community living in the camp also plays an active part in creating this reality, because the people want to live every moment of their lives to the hilt. They want to live as fully as possible, to retrieve the lost years of the war. There is definitely a feeling of elation.

I stay in Fernwald for only a short time. My health is very poor. The pneumonia I had in Carlsbad that wasn't treated in time, left me very weak and with spots on my lungs. After medical examinations, initiated by the *kibbutz* nurse, Goldmanowa, it is decided to send me to a sanatorium for lung diseases, in order to strengthen me. The sanatorium is located in Feldafing, a lovely mountain village in Bavaria. Several of the older survivors, with whom I had lived in the orphanage in Poland, are also sent there.

The Squirrel from Feldafing

I don't want to leave the other children – the members of my kibbutz in Fernwald. I don't want to leave the movement activities, the trips and the performances, which I cherish. It's also difficult for me to part with the new friends I made here. Besides which, my health problems don't exactly interest me and I don't understand their significance. But no one takes my desires into consideration. The leaders tell me that health comes before everything else, and I am sent to Feldafing against my will at the end of 1945, and placed in a German sanatorium for lung diseases. The nurses are German nuns and the entire medical staff are German. Most of the patients are also German, but there are several rooms reserved for Jews, Holocaust survivors. There are no Jewish children there, so I am placed in a room with two Hungarian Jewesses who are much older than I am. In the beginning I find it very difficult to adapt to the sanatorium and its atmosphere. There is no resemblance to the active *kibbutz* life I came from. However, with time I get used to the place and especially to my roommates. They play all sorts of games with me and try to teach me Hungarian, a task at which they fail dismally, but that I enjoy very much. I sing well in three languages, so I sing to them in Yiddish, Polish and in Russian. They like my songs and my voice and they enrich my repertoire with a few Hungarian songs, some of which I still remember.

The living conditions in the sanatorium are much better than those in Fernwald. I have space to myself, a clean bed not in the upper berth, rich food in accordance with my health needs and much serenity and rest, which seem unnecessary to me. I am bored. I can see a large fir tree from my window. A small brown squirrel that lives in the tree becomes the focus of my attention during my entire hospitalization. I spend hours watching the squirrel's activities and his play, and I become familiar with his way of life. The fir tree is large and covered with snow. The squirrel has a store of food among the tree's branches and this occupies him all the time. He goes in and out of there many times during the day, always clutching something in his front paws. He jumps from branch to branch with amazing speed. He climbs up and down the tree endlessly and his tail, which is twice his size, seems to be chasing him. The squirrel becomes my secret friend. From the moment I open my eyes in the morning I wait for him to appear and I share my experiences, my thoughts and my dreams with him. I anxiously await his return whenever he wanders off.

The sanatorium nurses, who are nuns, are dressed in black, wear starched white headdresses and look very stern. The white color doesn't soften their stern look. They always look somber and they stand erect as a pole. They don't radiate any warmth or affection and that disturbs me very much. They carry out their duties and serve us well, but they don't have personal contact with any one of us. I am the only child among all the adult patients, but that makes no difference to them and doesn't awaken in them any affection or fondness for me. I don't remember ever being honored by a smile from any of them. The atmosphere in the sanatorium is altogether cold and reserved, and if it weren't for the Jewish patients who are warm and loving, I don't think I would have survived.

In the sanatorium, in addition to the superior food, once a month we receive packages from the Joint Distribution Committee with, among other things, cigarettes and chocolate from American Army Surplus. I still remember the delicious taste of the chocolate. It is bitter chocolate that comes in thick, hard cubes. I divide it into daily rations so that it will last a long time. I keep the cube of the day in my mouth without chewing it, until it melts. In that way I extend the pleasure for as long as possible. Actually, I haven't tasted chocolate (or any other sweet) since the beginning of the war. I also find the cigarettes useful because there is a shortage of cigarettes in Germany. I have an album of photos given to me by a German photographer in exchange for my cigarettes. The photos are a reminder of the time I spent in Feldafing.

In the building opposite us there is a ward of men suffering from various lung diseases, among them are three young Jewish men who were in the senior group with me in the orphanage in Helenuwek, and who left Poland in the same group. In the sanatorium we become a multi-aged support group, whose members help one another. We try to spend our free time together. We take many walks in the snow-covered hills and enjoy the beauty of the landscape. If it's very cold we spend our time in the boy's ward, telling jokes or having intimate conversations about our past lives and our dreams for the future. One of the boys had a severe case of tuberculosis and died. We are all very upset by this and fearful of it happening to one of us. Only a week ago he was with us, hiking and telling jokes, and suddenly he's gone. It's very difficult for us to accept his death. It infuriates us that after successfully surviving the horrors of the war, he dies now. We bury him in the earth of Feldafing, on one of the hills we love to climb. We place a barbed wire fence around the grave, at the head of which flies a gigantic emblem of *Ha'Shomer Ha'Tzair*. That is Moniek's grave. I don't know his surname, or if there is anyone alive who remembers him, other than the small group hospitalized with him.

In Feldafing I find a *kibbutz* of *Ha'Shomer Ha'Tzair* and participate in their Friday night activities in which they welcome the Shabbat, sing and dance. I find several children my age, who become my good friends and help me, somewhat, to get through the period of hospitalization. I love to visit the *kibbutz,* love their joy of life and the homey atmosphere. I feel like one of them – loving and loved. My favorite expression of joy is singing and in the *kibbutz* I have that in abundance. I learn many Hebrew songs, and despite my not understanding the words at all, I sing them with enthusiasm and devotion. Ironically, I didn't understand the words of the songs even when I had learned Hebrew. That was because the words had been so distorted they sounded ridiculous and I had to learn them anew. In that period I didn't know any Hebrew. Although at home I had heard the holy language in prayers and I also sang songs in Hebrew, the meaning of the words was totally unknown to me. I often pray in my heart that there will be a miracle and I will master the Hebrew language during a dream. I want to wake up and know the language perfectly! Knowledge of the language seems vital to me for my future life, but unfortunately the miracle doesn't materialize, and not knowing the Hebrew language upsets me greatly.

During my many visits to the *kibbutz* I have the feeling that something secretive and very important is about to take place, but I don't know what it is. I remember my great excitement when my young friends, members of the *kibbutz* finally revealed the secret to me; their imminent illegal immigration. After the revelation of their most guarded secret, I feel that I truly am one of them. To this day, I've reverently kept the photograph of the first group, taken the day before they left the *kibbutz* in Feldafing to immigrate to Israel illegally. In the photo, one sees the Israeli flag and the *Ha'Shomer Ha'Tzair* banner fluttering at the head of the group. All the older members are dressed in the same festive clothes, and we youngsters, crowd into their shadow. The first group to immigrate was carefully chosen and included the best, smartest and healthiest of the youth in the *kibbutz.* It's a great honor to be included in that group, which is expected to go through hardships on their way. I'm very envious of them. Despite the many years that have passed since then, I still remember the group's departure as one of the most moving moments of my life. Only then I began to believe, for the first time, that the end of my wanderings was nearing an end – and that I too would eventually reach the land that would be my homeland.

In the sanatorium we are checked periodically to see if there is any improvement in our lungs. During one of these examinations carried out by a doctor and a nurse, I listen to the conversation between them and am appalled. The doctor explains to the nurse that the race theory has not always stood the test of reality. He uses me as a concrete example of this and says, "Look, her blue eyes and blonde hair misled the experts and there are probably many more like her who survived because of that". I find their conversation very frightening. I am afraid that they may want to carry out what the racial theories failed to do. I fear they might try to poison me by some means, perhaps with food, medicines, or drink. I begin to examine everything offered me – although I don't know what exactly I should look for. I refuse to touch anything that looks suspicious to me because of its color, its shape or its smell, including food and medicine. Therefore, instead of my health improving, it is deteriorating. I lose my faith in the people of the sanatorium and feel that I must escape as soon as possible. I go to the leader in *Feldafing kibbutz* and ask him to take me out of the sanatorium at all costs and tell him that it's a matter of life and death. I don't want to tell the leader why this is so important to me, fearing that he would laugh at me. However, I'm determined to get out of there. The leader isn't prepared or isn't able to fulfill my request, but I don't cease to implore him. In the end, when the *kibbutz* in Feldafing is reorganized according to age due to the immigration, all those of my age are moved to another place. Through the efforts of the leader, reinforced by my insistent nagging, I join the children being moved to Leipheim in Germany.

The Socks Patchers

I'm sent to a kibbutz of youngsters in Leipheim. Again I must adjust to a new place, new customs and new children. Again I must find my place among them. As in the previous places I had been in since the loss of my family, I look for someone I can love, and who will return that love. This isn't simple because all the children have already

made friends and are already connected in one way or another to
the leaders. Not having much choice, I decide to try my luck with
Leah, one of the leaders who appeals to me. Leah has a brother in
the *kibbutz.* I'm very jealous of him and try to keep him away from
his sister in every way possible. I devise all kinds of schemes to
keep Leah for myself. I want her only for myself. With time, Leah's
brother becomes one of my best friends.

Kibbutz life in Leipheim is independent, just as it was in Fernwald.
We cook, wash our clothes, conduct marches, go on hikes and
have ideological discussions about settling in Israel. The boys
are more courageous than the girls and wander around the city
without the accompaniment of the leaders. They look for surplus
army equipment to bring to Israel. There is an underground
aircraft factory in the city and in one the boys' searches they find
a revolver, which becomes our best-kept secret and the source
of much excitement. The leaders don't know about it, and two of
the boys smuggle it into Israel inside a loaf of bread. When we
come to *Kibbutz Gan Shmuel,* they keep it for a while, but when
the British army begins to conduct searches for arms, they give
it to the man in charge of the *kibbutz* armory.

I remember sitting outside with the girls, warming ourselves in
the spring sun, and patching the socks of all the children. We
compete with one another to see who can make the nicest patch.
There are several ways to do this, one of which is to sew in a
crisscross weaving pattern. If you invest enough time in this,
you can produce a patch so beautiful that it resembles a work
of art. I'm also one of the patch makers and even one of the

best, because I have previous experience, acquired while living with the Bacher family. A beautiful patch wins prestige to the seamstress, and this is an opportunity for me to improve my position with the other children.

I don't manage to make new friends or to acclimatize to Leipheim during the short period I spend there, and we are already getting prepared to move to a new place called "Jordenbad", a better place for children our age. I don't know who is in charge of this transport and why we are being moved, but we were told that this would be one of our last stations before immigrating to Israel. That magic sentence suffices to repress any tendency on our part to complain about constantly moving from one place to another. We don't give the leaders a hard time. We pack our belongings; we detach everything from the walls that might be of use to us in the new place and are ready to move. Actually the only permanent thing in our lives is the lack of permanence.

The Masculine Nuns
I don't remember how long the trip was, or where in Germany, Jordenbad is located, but I do remember a walled-in monastery, located in a beautiful and isolated area. Within the walls there are long, high, red-bricked buildings with many windows. There are vegetable gardens, fruit orchards and vast fields of grain. I am surprised to see nuns doing the difficult, physical work in each one of those places. They are doing work that is challenging even for men. They plough, harvest, pick fruit and vegetables, and carry heavy sacks on their backs; all this is done quietly and without difficulty. We are the first group of children our age to come to the

monastery. Many children arrived after us and there were already youth groups and adults living in the wings of the monastery. They are all waiting for their turn to immigrate, legally or illegally. None of these people works for their keep. We don't even have a duty rotation, as we were accustomed in our *kibbutzim*. It's like living in a convalescent home. There is a gigantic dining room in the monastery with long wooden tables and benches. The nuns serve us three meals a day, rushing between the tables like black ants, in order to answer all of our requests. I have a special feeling there: the knowledge that I am almost at the end of my long journey to Israel, combined with the breathtaking landscape surrounding us makes me feel wonderful in a way I haven't felt in a very long time. I walk about the gardens and the orchards enjoying the fragrance of spring. The good appetite I develop here, contributes much more to my health than all the time spent at the sanatorium.

Jordenbad serves as one of the last stations before immigrating to Israel – not only for us, but for all the many groups waiting in Germany to immigrate. There are frequent farewell parties for the groups leaving for Israel, and they include cultural and artistic programs that we prepare ourselves. Even I had the honor of appearing in a ballet performance that the girls from an older *kibbutz* laboriously taught me.

At the end of March 1946 the British Mandate Government made a special gesture to the Jewish people by contributing a thousand certificates for children survivors, and that was in addition to the White Paper quota. A certificate is the answer to the wishes of all those desiring to immigrate to Israel legally.

Since illegal immigration involves many difficulties and dangers, anyone able to immigrate legally feels ecstatic. I don't know who the privileged children will be, or who chooses the candidates. However, one day I am notified by the Secretariat of my group that they have no certificate for me and I will, therefore, not be immigrating with the rest of the group; I will be separated from them and from the leaders. I have become very attached to them over the course of time. The greatest disappointment is the delay in realizing my dream.

Actually, I don't really understand the essential difference between legal and illegal immigration and I am prepared to immigrate by any means offered me, but I want to arrive in Israel with my friends. I share my feelings with one of the children, Itzik Gottlieb, with whom I was very close, and who is my partner in life today. I remember the tears that streamed from my blue eyes, when I told him that I have no certificate and that I won't be immigrating with the rest of the group. We sit together on my bed, feeling sad about our friendship that is about to be cut off. I don't know if it was the friendship between Itzik and our leader's sister, Leah that helped me, or if it just happened, but just before the departure of the group to France, I am suddenly informed that a certificate was found for me, and I will be leaving with them. I am overjoyed. I jump up and down, I dance, I shout in every direction that I am immigrating to Israel with all the children of my group! I promise myself that as soon as I arrive in Israel I will try to reach Jerusalem, the place I always heard mentioned in my parents' prayers, and I will kiss the earth there in their name. I was the thousandth child, to join those gathered from the many displaced persons camps and privileged to leave the cursed land of Germany in the year 1946.

In 1990, on the anniversary of the exact date we had immigrated to Israel, Itzik and I visited Leah, our former leader. She was lying on her deathbed in Belinson Hospital and was very happy that we had remembered her past kindness and came to visit her. When I asked her if she was really the one who helped me immigrate with my group, it was already too late. In her condition, she wasn't able to recall such details from so long ago.

Passover in Marseille

The beginning of April 1946: I'm squashed in a truck loaded with children, which transporting us from Germany to France. My eyes hungrily take in everything around me. I'm overcome by excitement and foster hopes about what I will find in my cherished country. My greatest hope is to find a warm home where I'll feel welcome. The landscapes along the way are constantly being left behind and with them, the Diaspora. My enthusiasm is so great that I'm not certain if it's all a dream or reality. Suddenly I discern trees carrying golden fruit. I don't understand. I thought that oranges grew only in Israel, and I feel that they have no right to be growing in any other place. I have always believed that everything existing in Israel could not be found anywhere else in the world. I don't remember how long our journey was, but at the end we arrived at a gigantic camp with very many wooden buildings with curving roofs, resembling the Displaced Persons Camps of Germany. The place is bubbling with activity. Hordes of people are running about from one place to another, many of them with bundles in their arms, and this reminds me of the sight of the refugees that passed through our village at the beginning of the war. We are ushered into one of the long buildings and join in the general turmoil.

It's the height of spring, Passover Eve, and we are preparing a massive Passover *Seder* (ceremonial meal) in the camp of Marseilles. We assemble many long tables along the columns of trees and place wooden benches beside them. White tablecloths are spread on the tables and they look like bridal veils to me. Everything looks elegantly festive. The holiday of freedom being celebrated just before my immigration to Israel has great significance for me. It's a kind of personal Exodus from Egypt, from the Diaspora to Freedom. We are all very excited and we enthusiastically participate in the preparations for the holiday. We make ourselves available wherever help is needed. On the eve of the *Seder* I sort through my few raggedy clothes, to find the most festive garment I have. At home my mother always used to present me with a new dress and a gift on Passover Eve, because my birthday coincided with that date. At home the holiday always had an air of majesty for me, and something from that atmosphere and the need to be pretty and festive, suddenly awakens in me again in Marseilles. I feel the same elation and expectation that I used to feel before the holidays at home. I am ecstatic. I'm also very curious, because I have never participated in a Passover Seder with hundreds of people. I couldn't imagine how a Seder is conducted with so many people. To my great surprise the massive Seder is conducted very festively. There is much singing and reading from the Bible in Hebrew. The Haggadah is read as well, as we did at home, and the four questions are asked. There are many singing performances and community singing as well. I am especially moved by a little boy, standing on one of the tables so that he can be seen, and singing "And Perhaps" written by the Hebrew poetess, Rachel. He has the voice of a nightingale rising into the Heavens, and when he reaches the words, "Oh my Sea of Galilee", I am convinced that in the glittering evening sky of this Seder Eve, God is also listening to this wonderful song. The Seder goes on for many hours. People just don't want to leave this festive scene. Everyone feels emotionally moved and even after the official closing of the Seder, many people remain sitting on the lawn and singing. Tzvi Bar Niv, with his guitar and velvety voice, amazes us with his songs until the wee hours of the night. I'm sitting beside him. I feel that I'm in a dream; the way I felt during the singing at home on the Shabbat Eve. I feel I am floating higher and higher.

We must wait for the ship in Marseilles for twenty days. The leaders organize trips for us in the area. One of the first trips is to the seashore that is several kilometers from the camp. There, for the first time in my life, I see the ocean. I'm amazed to see such an infinite expanse of water. Wherever I look there is water and more water, as though there are no continents in the world, as though there is no end to the water. I've never even imagined such a sight. In stories I've heard, the ocean always ends somewhere, but now that I am looking at it, I don't see any end, any opposite shore. The ocean waves break forcefully against the rocky cliffs of the shore creating a gigantic spray of white foam. I imagine that the ocean is very angry with these cliffs, if it beats them so mercilessly. The sea attracts and frightens me with its power and wrath. I didn't know that Israel is bordered by the sea and will be very available to me, some ten minutes away from where I'll be living. From my village in Poland it would be necessary to travel hundreds of kilometers to reach the sea, therefore I never did. My parents didn't live long enough to show me the sea, just as they didn't manage to show me many other things they had planned for me.

The long awaited arrival of the ship is finally here, close to my thirteenth birthday, which falls on the tenth of April, according to the Gregorian calendar. We board the ship in great tumult and boundless joy. I am curious and worried about such an enormous structure floating on the water. I bring my belongings to the place allotted to me, and rush up to the deck. I want to see everything and to know everything about the frightening and endlessness sea, I want to understand how such a gigantic structure called a ship, floats on the surface of the water and doesn't sink. I ask myself what one does if, God forbid, the ship does sink! I don't know how to swim and will undoubtedly drown immediately. I don't dare tell anyone that I'm afraid of sailing on the sea. It's the only way to get to Israel, and to admit that I'm afraid of the trip seems to me like a betrayal of Zionism. The ship that took us to Israel was called "Champollion". I cried when it actually did sink several years ago. My warm sentiments for the ship have in no way faded with the years.

Our voyage on the Mediterranean takes two weeks and is peaceful and calm. Most of the time the sea is flat as a mirror. The sea and I celebrate my thirteenth birthday together. I feel that I'm undergoing a ritual of passing into adulthood. I feel that my personality has changed over the course of the voyage and that I have greater inner strength than I had before. Most of the passengers on the ship suffer from seasickness. They feel nauseous and dizzy and throw up everything they eat. I am fortunately one of the few who doesn't get sick. I spend much of my time on the deck helping other children who don't feel well. Some of my friends and I keep looking for stowaways who are said to be found on the ship hiding in wooden barrels. I was told about them, in great secrecy, by children in my group. The stories stimulate our imaginations and we are determined to find these stowaways at all cost. We behave like detectives in a storybook and look for them wherever our imaginations take us. However, we don't succeed in finding any. I don't know if there was any truth in those stories at all, but both my friends and I invested great efforts in trying to find them, and if they really were on the ship, they were very well hidden.

From horizon to horizon there is only water and a calm sea. We play, sing and sometimes have discussions with our leaders, but time passes slowly. When will we see the shores of our Promised Land? My tension increases from day to day, I don't have any more patience to wait. The ship sometimes stops at different ports. The only one I remember is the port of Alexandria. As soon as the ship anchors, a multitude of boats suddenly appear from the shore and race toward the ship. The boats carry peddlers who loudly call out the attributes of their wares. It is a fascinating sight. The different products in the boats create a mosaic of colors and the voices of the peddlers mix together into a jumble of sounds, a symphony of Eastern trills that I had never heard before.

According to the leaders, the ship is already very close to the shore of Israel and we still haven't learned how to sing our national anthem. The leaders decide to teach us the words of *Ha'Tikva* – word-by-word – so that we will be able to welcome the Israeli shore with the dignity the occasion deserves. I learn the melody quickly, but the words keep getting mixed up in my mouth. They don't have any meaning for me yet, because I don't understand the language. It is explained to me that this is the anthem of the Jewish people that expresses the longing for the Land of Israel. I accept it as a prayer in the Holy language, since my parents used to pray at home without understanding the contents of the prayer. I relate to the anthem with pride and reverence.

On the twenty-fifth of April, at three in the morning, the leaders wake us and tell us to go up to the deck in order to see the ship approaching the Israeli shore. In a short time, we suddenly see before us a wondrous sight: a gigantic brooch, inlaid with sparkling jewels, seems to rise from the sea, growing steadily and coming closer and closer. These are the lights of Mount Carmel in Haifa. The closer we come to the shore, the more fascinating the brooch becomes. Spontaneously, without any command, we all stand at attention and *Ha'Tikva* bursts forth from a thousand throats. It is a glorious sound, filled with emotion, a kind of festive Morning Prayer rising from our souls, which knew so much suffering and now yearn for a good, new life. With the coming of dawn the lights of Haifa grow dimmer, and when the sun rises we begin to see the silhouettes of the city's buildings. The ship anchors in Haifa port in the late hours of the morning. At about ten o'clock we leave the ship. In the port we are greeted warmly by a large crowd. They toss chocolate and oranges at us. The people of Haifa, who are waiting for us, know we are children who have survived the Holocaust. Some of them are holding signs with their family names. They hope to find relatives among us. We are not permitted to meet with the crowd waiting on the pier. Instead we are loaded onto a truck and brought directly to the transition camp in *Atlit*, due to the necessity of isolating us and spraying us with D.D.T. This was the customary procedure for new immigrants.

The Last Stop

In *Atlit*, we are again accommodated in wooden lodgings similar to those in the Displaced Persons Camps. We must be in isolation for a week, to prevent spreading contagious diseases we may have brought with us. We must be sprayed with D.D.T., examined for lice, and for general health. In addition, we have to be sorted according to age and our movement affiliation, before being sent to the places prepared for us. We accept all these procedures, some of which are unpleasant and even humiliating, with understanding and we don't complain. We believe this is the way we must be treated.

Finding places for a thousand children – who have nothing, is not a simple task. Most of us are orphans, and only a few of us have relatives in the country. Most of us haven't even had the minimal education expected for children our age. On the other hand, we do have a great deal of experience in fighting for our survival, knowledge we gained in the school of life. Many of us have a variety of problems that should be dealt with, but no one even takes that into consideration while making all these arrangements for us. Evidently, the struggle to create the new State, combined with a complete lack of understanding of what we had gone through, prevents Israeli institutions from relating to our emotional and physical problems.

I don't know based on what criteria the distribution of the children to different places was decided. We belonged to *Aliyat Ha'Noar,* but they didn't have any institutions capable of absorbing us. Actually, the *kibbutz* movement absorbed most of us, but not without many reservations. We, who had been educated in *Ha'Shomer Ha'Tzair,* were certain the *kibbutzim* of *Ha'Shomer Ha'Tzair* were anxious for us to come. Though from reading the minutes taken in the *kibbutz* general assemblies of that period, it becomes clear that this was not exactly what happened. During that period there were stormy discussions as to whether the *kibbutz* could afford to absorb the children survivors. The *kibbutz* children of our age went to a prestigious school in *Kibbutz Mishmar Haemek.* We were not meant to receive the same conditions as the *kibbutz* children, because *Aliyat Ha'Noar,* the institution responsible for our absorption into the country, did not have the funds to finance such an expensive education. The solution was *"Hevrat Ha'Noar"* (The Society of Youth) which included studies half a day and work half a day, thereby financing a good part of the expenses for our upkeep. As a work force, it was profitable for the *kibbutz* to absorb us, especially for work in the fields where many workers were needed at the same time.

I was informed that I am supposed to go to *Kibbutz Mesilot* with a group of children my age, which was randomly organized. I didn't know most of the children, and the idea that I would again be separated from the group I had been with all the way to Israel, and would have to begin everything anew, made me very unhappy. Had all my efforts to be one of the group been in vain?! I don't understand the calculations the *Aliyat Ha'Noar* make based on age. I am two years younger than the children in the group I immigrated with. This hadn't bothered anyone up to now, nor did it bother me. Why does it bother *Aliyat Ha'Noar* now? I feel it isn't fair and even a bit frightening, to be put in a situation where I begin a new life in a strange country with unfamiliar children, and without any knowledge of the spoken language. I cry incessantly and don't know to whom to turn for help. In Israel, in the new situation, our leaders have no influence and no ability to interfere. We are separated from them; they are in the same situation we are and are also distributed to different locations, and they, too, have personal problems adjusting to a new place and a new life.

One morning, as I stand outside my room, crying bitterly, a tall fatherly looking man approaches me and asks me why I'm crying. I open my heart to him without knowing that he is the *Ha'Shomer Ha'Tzair* representative in *Aliyat Ha'Noar,* Shmuel Shwartz, a member of *Kibbutz Mizra.* He listens earnestly and patiently. When I finish telling my story, he embraces me, thinks for a little while and says in a reassuring tone, "Remember my words! I will send you to the most beautiful, wealthiest, most secure and best place of all *Ha'Shomer Ha'Tzair kibbutzim* in the country. That place is *Kibbutz Gan Shmuel.* You will be with many more children than you were with before. I am certain that you will feel good there, and now, no more crying". He wipes my tears and looks deep into my eyes with a look that inspires faith, and then goes on his way. His words were very encouraging. They came from the depths of his heart and I believed him. I stop crying about my bitter fate. Fifty-three years have passed since then, and Shmuel Shwartz's description of my new home, *Gan Shmuel,* is still valid.

On the first of May in 1946, I arrive at *Gan Shmuel* with a group of children who will be in the same youth group with me. I am excited and curious about the place that will be my new home. After the warm welcome we receive in Haifa, we expect a joyous welcome in *Gan Shmuel* as well. To our disappointment, no one is expecting us in *Gan Shmuel* that day, and we are sent back to *Atlit.* The members of *Gan Shmuel* were participating in a mass May Day demonstration that day and there was no one there to greet us. We barely manage to step into a disinfectant pool against the hoof and mouth disease of the cows, and are loaded onto the truck and returned to *Atlit.* My first experience in my new home is very disappointing and arouses many doubts about the promises made by that good man in *Atlit.* I didn't know what the First of May was. We had never celebrated such a holiday at home, and I hadn't even heard about it. However, from the explanations we receive about not being welcomed in *Gan Shmuel,* I understand that it's a very important Israeli holiday that must be observed. On the way from *Atlit* to the *kibbutz,* I was very disappointed to see buildings, and not tents; green cultivated fields, and not wasteland; tall trees, flowers, bushes, and not a desert. I was angry and thought that the immigrants who came before us had already done everything that had to be done and didn't leave anything for us to contribute to the building the country.

The following day, on the second of May, we return to *Gan Shmuel*. This time are welcomed warmly by our future leaders and teachers, who in some ways will also be our foster parents. My geographical travels are over, but not my emotional journey. I make a great effort to integrate here, but in spite of my great love for the country, part of me is still there, where I was born, and that part of me will evidently remain there for as long as I live. All my loved ones are buried there, my happiest years were spent there, and I am still attached to the landscapes, the smells and memories of my childhood. I still miss the changing seasons, the smell of the lilac in the spring, the cherry tree in our yard, the stork's nest on the neighbor's roof, the shedding leaves of the chestnut trees in the fall, the snow painting the world white in the winter, and many other things for which I have found no substitute.

Epilogue

Fulfillment of My Oath

Seven years after the outbreak of the war I finally reach a permanent place, the country that is meant to become my homeland, and my home. The Hebrew language, the holy language of my parents, becomes the language of everyday conversation. I've reached a safe haven, but my longing for home doesn't cease. The more order and continuity there is in my life, the more I feel the absence of my family. I study, I work; I have a lively social life, I have very good friends, but all that belongs to the here and now, on the surface. What happens deep in my soul, I keep to myself. The most difficult times for me are the holidays and the Shabbat. Everything is so different here. At home everything was centered on the family, in the spirit of Jewish tradition, and here everything takes place within a large community, without religious ceremonies, and in a completely different atmosphere from that I experienced at home. In addition, I think constantly of the oath I made beside the grave where my family is buried, to keep the memory of my family alive, but I have no idea about how to go about it. In the world of the "new Jew", of heroic wars and of heroes, in a world that alienates the Diaspora Jew, how does one deal with a story like mine? How can I request

assistance in commemorating Jews who went to their deaths as
"sheep to slaughter"? I don't dare to speak to anyone about the
problem that weighs on me day and night. It also isn't customary
to talk about what we experienced during the war. No one asks
us what it was like, and evidently no one wants to hear about
it. Deep in my heart I know that I will fulfill my oath, but how?
These questions and a feeling of obligation are constantly on my
mind and I wait for an opportunity to fulfill that obligation and I
believe that it will come.

In the year 1955, nine years after my arrival in Israel, when I
already have a family and am the mother of a one-year old girl, I
hear about a festival of the World Democratic Youth, which will
take place in Warsaw, the capital of Poland. I decide that this is my
opportunity to try to reach Poland and to place a tombstone on
the communal grave in my native village. The Israeli delegation is
planning to participate with a performance using song and dance
to depict the building of the country. There are auditions held
for singers and dancers and I audition for singing. I'm overjoyed
when I am chosen to be the soloist of the choir. I know that as
a soloist, my chances are better for receiving permission from
the *kibbutz* to participate, than they would be if I were merely
one of the singers. Despite the difficulty in being separated from
my little daughter for an entire week, I make plans to realize my
dream of setting up a tombstone. I am hopelessly naïve. I think
that when I come to Poland, nothing will stand in my way. The
idea that perhaps I'll need money to carry out my plan doesn't
even occur to me. Since I am a member of a *kibbutz,* I have no
money of my own, and I don't talk about my plans to anyone in

the *kibbutz,* nor to anyone one in the Israeli delegation. I'm afraid that if they knew I had personal plans they might not accept me in the delegation.

When we arrive in Poland we meet with other delegations every day. The heads of our delegation arrange performances everywhere possible, so that Israel will be as visible as possible at the festival. We participate in the major performance of the festival, which ends very late at night, and there is no time for my private plans that motivated me to come here in the first place. Actually, I don't know who to approach and how to begin. On one of our few free mornings, I ask for help from the Jewish Community of Warsaw. I speak to the Head of the Community, tell him my story, and ask him if he can help me. It is a moving and promising conversation, at the end of which I leave a sketch of the location of the grave and the address of the place. He promises me that he will do his utmost to commemorate the grave. He explains that, in any event, this is the major occupation of the Community. Since there are very few living Jews left in Poland, the Community is mainly occupied with commemorating the dead. I leave the meeting with the head of the Jewish Community with many promises that seem credible, but nothing comes of them. He promises to arrange a visit in Wereszczyn for me, and nothing comes of that either. In order to go there I need to be accompanied by Russian soldiers to assure my safety. There is still a great deal of anti-Semitism, despite the fact that there are no Jews. A Jew appearing alone in that area would be in great danger.

Although I had visited Poland and I returned with a multitude of promises, I didn't succeed in accomplishing anything and I felt very frustrated. I knew deep in my heart that I would not rest until I had fulfilled my oath. I wait for another opportunity and it comes along only after thirty-two years.

A Trial Trip

In 1987 I have another opportunity to return to Poland. I'm appointed to present the products of the factory in which I work to the commercial companies of Communist Poland. These companies are financed by their government to purchase citrus fruit from our *kibbutz* factory. I then request of the factory management to allow me one day on my own, in order to make a trial trip to Wereszczyn, my native village. I decide that this time I will exploit the opportunity to find out how I can arrange a tombstone for the communal grave in the village, which I had vowed to do when I was nine years old. I am now much less naïve than I was on my first trip. I gather all the information I need beforehand. I make an advance arrangement for a group of four Polish people to accompany me to my native village. I contact Shmuel, who lives in Warsaw and has a sister in *Kibbutz Gan Shmuel.* He becomes my adviser and guide. I succeed in locating the Bacher family, and in recruiting one of the Bacher sons to assist me. In addition I recruit Yosef Cohen, the factory marketer and member of *Kibbutz Gan Shmuel,* who is with me in the factory delegation, and the Polish taxi driver, who is very sympathetic and friendly when I explain what the purpose of the trip is. The driver is a great help, because he is familiar with the customs of Communist Poland.

On the twenty-fifth of November in 1987, after our many advance preparations, (especially with regard to obtaining the necessary fuel), we set out early in the morning from Warsaw in the direction of Wereszczyn. A thin drizzle blurs the landscape seen through the windows of the cab. I'm deeply moved. The familiar smell of the Polish autumn brings me back to my youth. It's as though I am in a movie: I am both participant and observer. We pass through many places, the names of which I remember from my childhood. The first familiar city is the resort town of Otwock in the vicinity of Warsaw. Every Jew with a decent income used to go there for a summer vacation. My parents never could afford it. It took them time to become economically secure, and when they finally could afford a vacation, they were killed by the Germans.

We pass beside forests that I remember so well, and loved so much in my childhood that I can't restrain myself and request that we stop. I must go inside the forest to breathe in its smells, to touch the pine needles, wet with rain, to look for the berries I remember from my childhood. My Polish guides don't understand why I make such a fuss over each tree, bush and flower. For them these are common sights, and for me it's like going back in a time machine. This is the life I once had and has disappeared. We arrive in Lublin, one of the oldest cities of Poland, where Jews lived as early as the thirteenth century.

When we leave Lublin on the road leading to Wlodawa I remember the names of all the towns along the way. It's as though time has stopped. Everything has remained as it was. Only the Jews have disappeared. I am within the landscape of my childhood; the same trees; the same apple orchards; the same autumn smells that I loved. Everything looks as it did then. My delusional imagination and my memories bring tears to my eyes.

We are already in Urszulin, near the place where the German and Polish police stations used to be. I'm frightened. Visions from the past come back to haunt me. The Ukrainian soldier with his bayoneted rifle pointing at me suddenly appears before my eyes. I want to escape as quickly as possible from those harsh memories, and ask the driver to drive directly to Wereszczyn without stopping. My tension grows, the closer we come. What will I find there? Does the village still exist? Was it destroyed when the Germans retreated? Perhaps the place has changed so drastically that I won't be able to find anything. Meanwhile, the approach hasn't changed. The boulevard leading to the village looks the same. Even the trees look the same. I tell my guides that our house should be at the end of the boulevard we are traveling on. Does it still exist? "Here is our house", I shout, "It's still here, and has hardly changed at all". I realize that no one is waiting for me inside and decide not to stop there. I want first of all to get to the grave. To my sorrow, everything dear to me is found there. Almost nothing has changed, not even the path to the grave, and I lead the taxi there without the aid of the local guide. I don't believe what I see.

When I left the grave on the day of the massacre, there was a gigantic pile of earth, but now there is no earth and no pit. There is no sign of the grave, no markings indicating that it is the burial place of human beings. I shudder. How can it be that no tablet or stone marks this place so close to my heart?! Doesn't a Jew have any value in their eyes? Their well cared for cemetery is proof of their respect for the dead, but evidently only for the dead of their nationality and not those of the Jews. I recall that Kaddish has never been said for the memory of my family, and they probably expect me to attend to that. According to tradition, a woman is forbidden to say Kaddish. Fortunately, there are Jewish men with me and I will finally be able to fulfill that commandment. I am certain that this was the last wish of everyone buried in this grave. I ask Shmuel, the oldest man among us, to say Kaddish, the words of which are now heard here for the first time in forty-five years. I feel certain that they penetrate the seven heavens and that the souls of my dear ones are finally put to rest and receive their just rewards.

Entrance to the barn where Miriam hid the first night after the murders, the house is in the background 1987

Meanwhile, the driver finds an old local woman to verify my identity. When I tell her that I am Alter Zunszjan's daughter, she immediately knows who I am talking about. She remembers my parents and their shop very well. She also remembers the murder of my little brother. He was only four years old when he was killed and his death weighs heavily on my conscience all my life. I think that if I had been able to hold on to him when he struggled to get away, perhaps he would have survived. When the villagers notice the gathering of people near the hayloft, which is almost linked to the grave, they come to see what's going on. When they hear whose daughter I am, they rebuke me. Why did it take me so long to recall that my parents are buried here? Why didn't I arrange that someone place a tombstone or some other marking here? You're an ungrateful daughter. I am boiling with anger, but I say nothing. There is no point in trying to explain to them why it took me so long to get here. I also don't ask them why, over the course of forty-five years, no righteous one among them thought of placing some kind of mark, even a small stone, to indicate that human beings, inhabitants of the village, are buried here. Their reprimand is pure hypocrisy and I shouldn't let it upset me, but it does. I look for a large stone to place on the grave temporarily, until I can replace it with a tombstone. Politely, I request that the villagers do not move the stone. Tears are burning my throat, but I don't want to cry in their presence. I don't want to appear to be a pitiful, weak Jewess. I don't want their hypocritical sympathy. They haven't changed and I haven't forgotten anything. There is an old Polish woman living in the vicinity of the grave. She isn't one of the previous inhabitants and didn't know my family. The house she is living in didn't exist at the time of the massacre. I ask her if she agrees that I put up a tombstone on the grave and she answers that she has no objections on condition that the authorities don't object. When I ask her who the relevant authorities are, she directs me to the regional council in Urszulin. Since there is nothing else I can do here at the moment, I leave with a heavy heart.

Now, after having located the place of the grave, which is actually all that is left of my home, I invite my guides to come with me to the house I grew up in. The house itself hasn't changed much, but it's been extremely neglected. There are no signs that anyone had tried to preserve it during the forty-five years that have passed since then. I am told that the tenants change frequently and that there is no explanation for this. The well that I used to drink from and that I would look into curiously and a bit fearfully, to see its far away bottom, still stands in the yard. It looks much smaller than I remember it.

The well in the garden at the house, 1987

When I left at the age of nine, my shoulders barely reached the opening, and now it barely reaches my knees. Everything is so much the same and so different from what it once was.

The house in 1987, taken during the first trip back to Poland.

The site of the mass grave of the Jews of **Wereszczyn**
located next to the barn. (Photo taken in 1987.)

Today my eyes probably see differently from the way they did when I was a child. I am very excited. Scenes from my happy childhood appear to me at every turn. My father, my mother, my grandmother and my two little brothers are here now with me. I sense their presence everywhere. I fantasize that I am again a little girl, living in the house I loved and my whole family is with me. My eyes search every corner and seek out what there once was. Suddenly, my vision of the past vanishes and I find myself back in the present. This causes me great physical and mental pain. My legs turn to stone and I am barely able to move. In a half whisper I say to Yosef Cohen, a member of my *kibbutz*, "You see, Yosele, I also once had a home and it was here. I had a mother and a father. I had a loving family, and in this yard that we are standing in now, I experienced many happy hours. I wasn't born from stone. I was also born to a woman".

In my present home, *Gan Shmuel*, no one knows my family and my past and perhaps they don't know me as I really am. I, like many others who were left without relatives, often feel uprooted and homeless, without any witnesses of our former lives. Some of us are still trying to find out where they came from and what their names were. I, too, know almost nothing about my extended family. I never even met them because most of them lived in far-off places in Poland and were killed before I ever met them. Just recently I learned from my cousin, who is older than I am, that my mother had eleven brothers and sisters from the two marriages of her father, and I knew nothing about this.

Time is running out and if I want to attend to the issue of the tombstone, I must leave the home and landscape of my childhood, and go to the regional council in Urszulin and meet the administrator. Before leaving the place, I go to a corner of the yard, where our box of gold was buried. The place was dug up a short time after the massacre and the gold was stolen. I joked on the way here about the possibility of becoming rich, but now it's clear to me that I won't. Our driver asks one of the local people about gold, and the villager verifies the fact that they found the gold immediately after the massacre. We leave the villagers and the village and head for Urszulin. I am torn between the desire to remain and see more, and the need to move on.

It takes us a while to find the Council building. The Head of the Council, a young man in his thirties, greets us cordially and asks how he can help us. When I tell him my story, he is amazed. He never knew that Jews had ever lived in that area. He hears about the common grave in Wereszczyn for the first time. He had also never heard that Jews had once lived in Urszulin. Despite the witnesses I have that Wereszczyn was my birthplace, and despite the fact that there are people there today who remember me, and my family, he is unable to permit me to set up a memorial, only on the basis of my story. He is obliged to confirm my story through an extensive examination in the upper echelons of the government. We leave him a nice gift and take our leave. We are heading back to Warsaw. I am again immersed in my own small world. Will there be any substantial results from this visit to Poland? Will I succeed in moving something in the People's Democracy of Poland so that they will permit me to do something that had not been acceptable in the past? Who else must I approach in order to succeed?

We return to Warsaw by way of the city, Kazimierz Dolny. It is twilight. On the slope of a hill to the side of the road, there is a huge memorial wall made up of tombstones that had been torn from their graves and used to pave sidewalks. Kazimierz Dolny is a lovely summer resort on the banks of the Wisla River that had been inhabited only by Jews before the war. The city was not harmed during the war and the king's palace, built on the side of a mountain, continues to overlook the houses of the city. Everything looks almost the same as it was, except that, again, the Jews have disappeared. The synagogue is being used as a cinema, and its previous use is recognizable only by the shape of the building. The beautiful town square beside the synagogue is still buzzing with life, but the people are all Polish. There is no trace of the merchants, the craftsmen, or the Yeshiva students who once populated the square. They continue to live only on the wall of tombstones. I read the epitaphs on the wall and the life of the city is revived before my eyes. The symbols on the tombstones indicate the occupations of those buried there. There had been so much activity, so much life. An entire world has disappeared. I light a memorial candle beside the wall of tombstones, and in answer to my request, Shmuel says *Kaddish* here as well.

We leave the place in silence; each of us immersed in his own reflections. One more night in Poland and I return home. We return to Warsaw at night. Warsaw, the capital of Poland,

which had once been considered the Paris of Eastern Europe,
is now grey, neglected and as quiet as an outlying rural town.
It's impossible to find even one coffeehouse open at night. Its
streets are empty and sad. I am not sorry to be leaving Poland.
The country saddens me, both as a human being and as a Jew.
I am probably not objective, but Poland, without the Jews who
lived here, seems lifeless. Jewish life is apparent now only in the
few cemeteries that haven't been destroyed.

The Second Journey

I wait for any sort of response from the Regional Council in
Poland, but I don't rest on my laurels. I look for contacts in Israel
and in Poland who could be of assistance. I ask Stephan Grajek,
the International Chairman of the Jewish Partisans, who has
good connections in Poland, to help me and perhaps, to issue my
request through official channels. After a thorough discussion
with him, I understand that if he applies officially, it will take
years to implement and there is no hope of receiving financial
support. I understand that I must work alone. Nevertheless, I
succeed in contacting Jan Jagielski, a Polish man dedicated to
the cause of preserving the remains of Jewish culture in Poland.
He is a wonderful person in every way, and reminds me of the
righteous people I met throughout my life, during and after
the war. He promises to help as much as he can. Shmuel, who
lives in Warsaw and is a retired general of the Polish army, also
continues to use his connections to assist me.

In the beginning of the summer of 1988 I receive a letter from
the Polish Government Authority for Memorials, including a

permit to build a memorial site in Wereszczyn. Documents had been found, which verified my story about the massacre of the Jews there, I send copies of the permit to Poland, to all those involved in the issue, in order to begin the actual work. I agree to take responsibility for all expenses, and ask Jan Jagielski to go to the Regional Council of Urszulin and also to Wereszczyn in order to set the process in motion. He and Shmuel go there and try to find the quickest way to go ahead with the project.

In the meantime, Jan Jagielski comes to Israel as a guest of *"Yad Vashem"*) the Israeli Holocaust Memorial Authority), and I consult with him about the tombstone. I am not certain what kind of site it should be. I don't want to build something that would disturb the local people, but I do want it to be satisfying for me. Jan says that the more modest it is, the less it will tempt the neighbors to destroy it. Marble might be stolen, and it is also very complicated to transport to such a remote place. The same is true of bringing stones. After consulting with Jan, I decide to prepare the tombstone in Israel, make it out of copper with a fitting epitaph in Hebrew and in Polish, and send it to Poland to be attached to the cement wall already standing in place. In August of 1988, I receive an invitation from the Regional Council of Urszulin, to come and officially consecrate the tombstone. On the thirtieth of August 1988, I fly to Poland in order to be there on the fourth of September for the unveiling of the tombstone in Wereszczyn.

I land in Warsaw. The city is grey and cold; it is raining and my mood is in keeping with the weather. I feel so alone. The plane lands exactly on time, but it is impossible to disembark from the airplane. There are no buses to take us to the arrival hall. Most of the passengers on the plane speak Hebrew, and I feel at ease among them, despite the fact that I'm not acquainted with any of them. We have a common fate; most of us are Jews and the past of each one of us is connected – in some way – to Poland, a country for which we have mixed feelings; happy memories as well as memories of suffering and hate. The buses arrive and we are finally able to get off the plane. Outside it is raining heavily and it is very cold. I am suddenly overcome by a longing for Israel, longing for the sun, for our blue skies, for the Israeli warmth and light. I momentarily regret having come. Why did I come? Who will care about this tombstone, even if I finally succeed in erecting it? Who will take care of it? I quickly shake off this feeling. I have a weighty, long-standing obligation and I must fulfill it.

I'm anxious because I don't know the people who are supposed to meet me at the airport. Since I've been delayed, they may have left the airport, and then I'll be completely lost. Fortunately, Jan Jagielski comes to meet me, instead of the other people, and he is waiting faithfully. We order a cab. The streets are drab, the houses covered with soot and the trees are beginning to shed their leaves. The smell of autumn brings back memories. I'm very tense and Jagielski tries to comfort me, but I'm incapable of shaking off this inexplicable anxiety. We come to Mokotowska Street, Shmuel's house. He is visiting in Israel. His daughter, Tereza takes me in. She has never seen me before and doesn't know the reason for my coming. She's very energetic and substantive, and tries hard to make me feel at home. We become acquainted while having our tea together and I tell her why I came to Poland, and how her father and I are connected. As soon as she becomes aware of the aim of my visit, she jumps up from her chair and brings me a letter that had just arrived from the Regional Council of Urszulin. I give it to Jagielski and he reads it to me. When I hear the contents, I almost go out of my mind. It appears that the woman who lives near the site of the grave, doesn't own the land. The land belongs to her sister and she hasn't allowed the workers to begin erecting the tombstone. The sister sensed the smell of Jewish money and she is determined to exploit the opportunity. Jagielski is furious. He feels humiliated and betrayed and doesn't know how to apologize to me. The Regional Council misled him and he summoned me to come to Poland in vain. I understand that all my efforts were in vain and that I was summoned to come at the wrong time.

We request a meeting the next day with the Regional Council in Urszulin in order to clarify what the exact situation is, and how we can continue the project. I recruit Tereza, Shmuel's daughter and her friend, Marta as reinforcements, in order to strengthen our delegation and our bargaining power. Marta is aggressive and fiesty. At six in the morning we are at the Warsaw train station with prearranged tickets, because this, too, is a complex undertaking in the current regime. Jagielski is already waiting for us at the station, and we forcefully push our way into the train in order to find seats. It's a long trip and the train is completely packed. I am so tense that I pay no attention to what is happening around me.

LIKE BIRDS IN BLACK AND WHITE

When we had set out on our way, the sky was grey and it was raining, but now the clouds have completely dispersed, the sun is warm and spreads its rays over everything. Only the faces of the people around us maintain their grayish color. Again we pass through the landscape of my childhood. We travel along the road that my father often traveled during his life, and I try to imagine him. Today I am more than twice as old as he was. He was only twenty-eight when he was killed. So many things appear strange to me. In a normal world parents are usually older than their children. With us it's just the opposite.

We finally arrive in Urszulin and visit the Regional Council. The Head of the Council had left before our arrival. It was evidently intentional. He knew we were coming. The meeting was arranged with him by phone. The clerk replacing him, maintained that he had heard about the issue of the monument and that the ceremony would take place as planned on Sunday, meaning tomorrow. I invite him to travel with us to Wereszczyn in order to verify this information. I am extremely tense and expect the worst. We arrive in Wereszczyn and go immediately to the grave, but there is nothing there. The area is covered with weeds and there is a large pile of sand next to the grave, indicating some attempt to do something, but there is no sign of cement. The clerk has no explanation for the absence of the tombstone we are supposed to consecrate tomorrow. He returns us to the Regional Council. Perhaps they have an explanation. It appears that he truly has no idea what is going on. At the Regional Council we learn that there is a problem. We are told to go to the owner of the land, who is holding up the proceedings. At this point everything depends on her. We learn that the land in question belongs to a farm woman from Weresczyn and not to her sister who lives on the land. We can't do anything without her permission. The head of the regional council is afraid of her violent family and won't do anything she doesn't agree to. Even the official, government issued permits to erect the tombstone are of no use in this instance.

I ask the clerk to take me to the landlady in order to clarify the issue with her. He takes us there very unwillingly. It's clear that he is not fond of the people he is taking us to meet. We arrive at a large house with a wide yard and a large dairy. Two automobiles are parked in the driveway, a rare thing for those days in Poland. It's clear that we are dealing with a very well-to-do family. The owner's daughter-in-law greets us outside. When we ask her why the erection of the tombstone is being delayed, she answers that she knows why, but she is not the spokesman for the family and her mother-in-law must be called from the fields. Her mother-in-law is the direct heir of the land in Wereszczyn, and only she can determine the conditions of anything done on her land. We wait for the mother-in-law and after a while a woman of large dimensions appears and without responding to our greetings, stands before us in a belligerent stance and informs us, "If you want to erect a tombstone on my land, you will have to pay for it! Neither the regional council nor the government will build anything on my land without my permission. I didn't allow the workers to start working, and my sons will destroy every drop of cement you

try to pour there. You will pay well for every inch of my land!"
I don't interfere, because I'm not able to speak. Suddenly she
asks me, "To which of the Jewish families in Wereszczyn do you
belong?" When I tell her whose daughter I am, she remembers
that at the time the Germans gathered all the Jews together in
the square, I had come to her looking for refuge, but she didn't
remember what happened after that. She reminds me that her
name is Helenka and that we played Hopscotch together as
children. I tremble. I recall pleading with her parents to hide
me. Evidently memories from those days are not especially
disturbing for her. She profited from our misfortune and from
the misfortune of many others and was able to increase her
property. She wants to include her husband and sons in the
discussion and sends us to them.

We accompany her to the place where apples are being picked,
some twenty kilometers from Urszulin in order to meet the father
of the family and his son who are supposed to determine the price
to be paid. We wait about twenty minutes for their lordships to
appear. The father comes first. He is polite, greets us cordially, and
even wishes to kiss my hand as is the custom in Poland. I pretend I
don't understand his intention and evade his kiss. He ingratiatingly
explains to us that after consulting with his son, he is charging
half a million zloty for the piece of land, and won't accept anything
less. Jagielski and the two Polish men with me are in shock when
they hear the sum. Jagielski is furious and tells them that they
are dealing in blood money and that he, as a Pole, is ashamed
for them. However, nothing moves them from their stand. The
husband says that it all depends on his wife. We have to negotiate

with her and that is a difficult task. On our return, the daughter-in-law tells her the sum decided upon, and my childhood friend is unwilling to accept anything less than that. "If there is no money, there is no tombstone. What difference does it make to me that Jews are buried here? The land is mine and I determine what will be on it!" Jagielski and Marta bargain with her and I say nothing, because if I were to open my mouth I would burst into tears, and I'm not prepared to give this scum the satisfaction of seeing me in my weakness. After long and tiring negotiations, Jagielski is prepared to sign a contract for a quarter of a million zloty and to wind up the agreement. He knows that it is the greatest amount I am capable of recruiting. When the landlady understands that I don't have half a million zloty, and that if she insists on that sum, the whole transaction will be cancelled and she won't gain anything, she is prepared to compromise.

After the signing of the agreement, we take the permit to the stonemason in Wereszczyn. It's already late in the day and we want to organize the beginning of the casting on the same day. The stonemason isn't there, but we manage to locate his sons, who are also stonemasons. They show us the wooden model their father had prepared for the tombstone, and the sacks of cement standing ready. They explain that they were unable to begin working because Helenka and her family threatened to break their bones if they began to do anything in that location. We show them the building permit we received from the landlords, but they can't do anything without their father. We drive to the person who is going to build the fence around the tombstone and he is very accommodating. I request that he put up the fence as soon as the cement is poured, so that I will manage to see it before my return home. I finally see my dream beginning to become a reality, at least partially.

I am again in Warsaw with the two partially Polish women, Tereza and Marta. They both decide to take me out of the house and cheer me up a bit by showing me the city. They both come from mixed families and both of them have some hidden connection to Judaism, which in turn creates a hidden connection with me, as well. They feel ashamed of the ugly bargaining I experienced in the village, and are apologetic about it, although they had tried to help me in every way possible.

Since it is Friday today, I ask Marta to take me to the synagogue to meet any Jews that might still exist. To my great surprise, she takes out a Hebrew booklet with all the important prayers, and the times for lighting candles. I am both confused and moved to tears by the strange mixture in this woman. She's proud of being Polish, but she also has a warm Jewish soul. I translate parts of the prayers in the booklet for her and both of us are deeply impressed by their beauty. Despite the fact that I don't observe the commandments, I feel elated by the prayers. I am much more Jewish here than I am in Israel. We go to the synagogue and I'm tense. In Warsaw I expect to meet at least a quorum of Jews on Shabbat Eve. We reach the synagogue and there is no one there. Another Israeli couple arrives for the same reason we came. After an exacting search in the area, we find the caretaker of the synagogue, who is willing to do us a special favor and allow us inside. Before the war, the wealthy Norzyk family privately owned this synagogue. Of all the many synagogues that were in Warsaw before the war, this is the only one that remained unharmed and is even active at times.

We go to sleep early because the next day is Saturday and we're expecting a long and tiring day. I decide to go to Wereszczyn on Saturday and not on Sunday as prearranged. I want to surprise the workers of the regional council during their workday, and to officially purchase the land surrounding the grave. I also want to officially finalize arrangements for the erection of the tombstone and the surrounding fence. I learned the hard way that if I come on Sunday – when expected – I won't find anyone with the necessary authority. Saturday morning there is a pouring rain. Outside, it is grey and cold, almost like my soul. Will I succeed this time in fulfilling my oath, or will I still be confronted by a blank wall? I am tense and anxious. How much strength will it take to realize my mission? What will I do if I again find nothing there?! Jagielski is waiting for us at the Warsaw train station, with tickets in his hand, and we run to the far end of the platform in the hope of finding places to sit. It is more crowded than it was on our previous trips, evidently because this is a weekend. We are pushed into a car where four obese men are seated, on their way home from work in West Germany. They praise Germany ceaselessly, drink vodka followed by choice German sausage, and continuously complain about Poland. Time is moving very slowly. I don't have the patience to wait. I'm anxious to see what has already been done.

We reach Lublin and rush to get a place in line for a taxi. However, this time, contrary to the previous situations, and perhaps due to the rain, there are many free cabs and not many people waiting. Within minutes, we are on our way. Every minute is valuable because the Regional Council closes at one o'clock, and we want to make all the arrangements before closing time. Due to the pouring rain, the cab is barely able to advance. Mud is smeared on the windows, blurring our vision in all directions. I am enclosed within my shell. My memories, my doubts, my pain; all intermingle, including a feeling of hate, which is very rare for me. I don't know how to hate, and that often makes me angry with myself. Finally, we reach Urszhulin and Head for the Regional Council. Fortunately, the office is still open and we are greeted by the Vice Head of the Council. He provides us with a certificate of ownership of the land surrounding the grave and we take that to Helenka's family, hoping that we'll find her at home and will be able to finalize the transaction. We surprise them, since we were supposed to come the following day. Their first question when we arrive is if we brought all the money. My positive answer brings a gleam into her eyes. Her wishes were granted. I read her the document I brought with me and request her signature. She still hesitates a bit, but the pile of bills in my hand is much more convincing than any words. Helenka signs and I feel relieved. Actually, at that moment, I cut myself off from them and enfold myself in my private world. The oath I made at the age of nine is finally becoming a reality. While Helenka's entire family is counting the money, happy that such a treasure has fallen into their hands with such ease, we leave the house on our way to completing our mission. We travel to Wereszczyn to see what the workers have achieved. We arrive at the grave and the place looks completely different from what it was like two days ago. The foundation is cast, iron poles have been placed all around it for protection, and the surrounding fence is already set up. The site is developing and looks very dignified.

The mass grave after the building of the memorial monument

Finally, after forty-six years, my family and the other Jews of my village are being honored with a tombstone, which I wanted so much to provide for them! Their bones are no longer scattered like forgotten rubbish. A monument will stand over their grave and an epitaph, written in their Holy language, Hebrew, will be a reminder of their existence and the date of their murder. Now, I am certain that I have really succeeded in fulfilling my oath. I will have to leave Poland without seeing the finished monument, but it will be completed despite my absence. All the anger, expectations, the sadness and the memories locked within me for so long, come bursting forth in a loud scream that I have no control over. Uncontrollable tears come pouring forth. Jagielski, my angel who constantly supports me and stands by me, takes a prayer book out of his pocket and says "Kaddish" (prayer for the deceased) in fluent Hebrew, on the background of continual bursts of tears. Tereza assures me that every year on the fourteenth of May, the anniversary of the massacre, she will come here to light a candle in their memory. I believe that she will really do that if she can.

We go to the home of the head construction worker to pay him part of the sum due for his work. He will receive the remainder of the sum when the work is completed. His family receives us warmly and apologizes to us in the name of many of the villagers, for the landlady's behavior. They tell us that not all the Polish people are greedy for money and hard-hearted as she is. He promises me to complete the work even in my absence and that I have nothing to worry about. I believe that he will keep his promise. We also pay the fence builder and I thank him from the bottom of my heart for his humanity towards me, and for his devotion to the work. He promises me to build such an invincible fence that no one will be able to damage it. I ask him to try to foster a favorable attitude towards my monument among the villagers, so that no one will do it any harm. Our mission is almost complete, and we make ready to leave Wereszczyn. However, I am strongly drawn to this grave and am unable to detach myself from it. My beloved mother, my dear father, my little brothers, my sweet grandmother, who was younger than I am today when she was killed, have you found peace and rest now? It is so hard for me to part from you. If it weren't for my family waiting for me in Israel, I think I would remain here to lie down beside you until my soul leaves my body and I can join you. Farewell to your dust, my dear ones. May your memory be blessed.

A Resurrection Torch – with WIZO (Women's International Zionist Organization)

The monument was erected and the Regional Council even conducted a ceremony for the unveiling, but I still haven't seen how it looks. When I return home, I feel I must tell the story of the monument. That's the only way I can commemorate my dear ones here in my homeland. I do this through television, on Ram Oren's program, "This is the Time". My story deeply touches many people in the country. Many survivors ask me to offer them advice on how to commemorate their relatives. My telephone doesn't stop ringing for weeks. I become a 'confessional priest' for survivors who didn't dare talk about their past beforehand. There are offers of monetary donations to help me with the completion of the monument, and there are also newspapers that offer to finance a trip to Poland for me, in exchange for an article in their newspaper. I decidedly refuse the offers of money, and also the request of the newspaper. I don't intend to make a scoop of the monument. That was not my purpose in appearing on television. However when the leading women of WIZO invite me to serve as a witness on their trips to Poland with Israeli youth, I accept their invitation. The purpose of the trip is to show the young women the remains of the Holocaust in Poland, and the place where the major annihilation of a large portion of the Jewish people took place. I agree to join them and I see the expedition as a mission. I want the young people to hear about the German conquest directly from me, and I want to see and to show the completed monument standing in its place. I request permission to bring my son, Eldar, with me so that someone from the next generation of my family will be able to take care of the place and say "Kaddish" there after I'm gone.

In May 1989 I'm in Poland for the third time within three years. I'm the guest of WIZO and serve as a living witness. However, at the last minute, I decide not to bring them to Wereszczyn. I'm afraid that if I bring a large group of Jews there, the local people might destroy the monument. They are engraved in my memory as Jew haters, and I therefore decide to go there with a limited team. I go there only with my son, Eldar, and WIZO's television team. Now again, I am on my way to Wereszczyn, but this time, not as the only remnant of my family. Eldar sits next to me. He is the continuing link in the chain. I have someone to whom I can pass on my heritage. The others accompanying us serve as witnesses to the fact that we existed and continue to exist. Along the way I tell my son all my experiences here that had been stored away in my memory. On arriving in Wereszczyn, we go directly to the monument and see that it is really standing in place, alone and orphaned at the end of the village, on the background of the hayloft and the vast cornfield surrounding it.

Students from "Oshrat" educational institution, at the house in 1990 –
During their trip to Poland. Miriam accompanied the group to bear witness.

The Monument to the Memory of the Jews of
Wereszczyn and the members of Miriam's family

It is modest and not conspicuous, like the Jews who lived
here and tried not to be offensive to the Gentiles. I am deeply,
deeply moved. I have realized my dream. My dear son is
standing beside me and, with his own eyes, sees the place
I've been telling him about since he was a little boy. Both
of us cry for our dead. My children never knew the taste of
life in an extended family. They never knew what it was like
to live with uncles and aunts, and to enjoy the pampering
of grandparents. All of them are buried here, where we now

stand. I am not a religious woman and none of my children are among the believers, but they honor my religious past and continue many of the traditional customs that were practiced in my home. I have a prayer book with me and ask my son to say *Kaddish* for our dead kinsmen buried here. My son, Eldar, is saying *Kaddish!* Papa, Mama, do you hear him? Your grandson, Henia and Alter, the grandson who was born in Israel, my loved ones, is saying *Kaddish* to redeem your souls. I hope that just as I have been your spokesman until now, they will continue when I am gone, and their children after them forever and ever.

A Personal Note

Even after that journey I found no peace, and it seems that I never shall. I haven't achieved peace of mind. I thought that after fulfilling my oath I would feel relieved and would no longer be troubled by the thought of that place. However there is a powerful bond connecting me to the inhabitants of that grave, a kind of umbilical cord that is impossible to sever. The bond grows stronger as I grow older. My obligation to serve my dead loved ones haunts me all the time. I've already taken two groups of Israeli youth, who were on a tour of the Holocaust sites in Poland, to see the grave. Now I have eighty more witnesses to the existence of those buried there, but that isn't enough. I will continue to tell their story so long as I live. If I could grow wings, I would fly around the whole world, telling the story of how they died. There is still so much oppression, racism and pointless wars which bring me back to those days, I feel the urge to shout a warning about human evil, and I hope that the story of a little girl who suffered so much only because of her descent, will make a small contribution in preventing such horrors from repeating themselves.

I have already lived in Israel fifty-four years. I love the country and my *kibbutz* home with all my heart. I've raised a model family; I have three children and seven grandchildren, all of whom are beautiful and talented. My beloved family is my personal victory over the Nazis, but still – part of me remains there, with my departed loved ones.

The words written above have been drawn from the depths of my tortured memory. They were written throughout the years on bits of paper here and there, on various occasions and in varying circumstances and then hidden away for many years. I hope that if my words are ever printed for all to read, that they will serve as further firsthand evidence of the ability of human beings, even the highly enlightened and cultured ones, to behave like beasts. It's also important for me to point out that despite all the evil I have met in my harsh past, I have also learned that even in the most iniquitous of places, there is always a handful of righteous people who are willing to endanger their own lives in order to save others. I shall never forget those good people who crossed my path when I was struggling to survive. They were my hope and my light in the darkness. Everyone, who survived the Holocaust, came across them, at one time or another, during his struggle for survival. I also have them to thank for my survival.

A memorial ceremony at the site of the memorial monument, with the participation of students from the educational institution, "Oshrat."

To those whose hearts have been touched by my story, I would like to request that if you happen to be in the vicinity of Lublin in Poland, please travel another sixty kilometers to a small village, called Wereszczyn, approach the tombstone standing at the edge of the village, near the hayloft, behind the church and the Christian cemetery, and say *Kaddish* for my loved ones. I thank you in advance from the bottom of my heart.

December 2001   Miriam Raz-Zunszajn

32602947R00155

Made in the USA
Middletown, DE
10 June 2016